PASTOR HALL
and
BLIND MAN'S BUFF

OTHER BOOKS AND PLAYS BY ERNST TOLLER

LEARN FROM MY YOUTH (I WAS A GERMAN)

LOOK THROUGH THE BARS

THE SWALLOW BOOK

NO MORE PEACE

SEVEN PLAYS

Pastor Hall

BY ERNST TOLLER

Translated from the German by Stephen Spender & Hugh Hunt

Blind Man's Buff

BY ERNST TOLLER

AND

DENIS JOHNSTON

RANDOM HOUSE · NEW YORK

PT 2642
.O65 P32
1939

DEDICATED TO THE DAY
WHEN THIS PLAY MAY BE
PERFORMED IN GERMANY

PASTOR HALL

CHARACTERS

FRIEDRICH HALL, Pastor

IDA HALL, his wife

CHRISTINE HALL, their daughter

GENERAL PAUL VON GROTJAHN, retired

DR. WERNER VON GROTJAHN, his son

FRITZ GERTE, Sturmbann leader, later Commandant in the Concentration Camp

JULIE, servant in the Rectory

TRAUGOTT PIPERMANN, a shoemaker

EGON FREUNDLICH

ERWIN KOHN

PETER HOFER

AUGUST KARSCH } Prisoners in the Concentration Camp

HERMANN STETLER

KARL MULLER

JOHANN HERDER

HEINRICH DEGEN, S. S. Man

JOSEPH LUEDEKE, Land Corporal } Guards in the Camp

Two officers of the Gestapo in uniform

SCENES

ACT ONE

ACT ONE

The stage is divided horizontally into a front room and a rear room. The rear room is a step higher than the front room, connected to it by sliding doors with large glass windows.

The living room in front is comfortably and unfashionably furnished. Behind, in the dining room, the table is festively decorated and prepared for the evening meal.

When the curtain goes up, IDA HALL *is arranging flowers in the dining room. She changes vases around and takes good care that the colors of the flowers "harmonize."*

IDA HALL *is a woman of about forty, young-looking, with blonde hair wound in a bun. Her gestures are changeable, her eyes wander anxiously around.*

JULIE *comes in.*

JULIE: Frau Pastor, Stormtroop Leader Gerte wants to see you.

IDA HALL (*surprised*): What does he want, Julie?

JULIE: He didn't say, Frau Pastor.

IDA HALL (*glancing at the clock*): Quarter past seven and dinner at eight. . . . Did you tell him we are expecting guests?

JULIE: He said it was urgent.

IDA HALL: Very well. Show him in. (*Julie goes toward the door, Ida calls her back*) And, Julie, tell cook not to oversalt the roast, General Grotjahn is so particular.

JULIE: Very well, Frau Pastor.

IDA HALL: Is the pastor not back yet?

JULIE: He went out to visit the Enkels. Their little daughter, the one that went to the labor camp, is going to have a baby.

IDA HALL: You mean Lilly? But she's only fourteen—well, we mustn't concern ourselves with these things. Go and ask the Stormtroop Leader to come in, he doesn't like being kept waiting.

7

JULIE: Frau Pastor, if I might say something . . .

IDA HALL: Well?

JULIE: It's about the Herr Pastor. . . . (*She finds it hard to continue. Ida Hall looks at her for a moment.*)

IDA HALL: No, Julie, not now. You have been very faithful to us for a long time, but I won't allow the servants to discuss the master either with me or behind his back. What Pastor Hall does is no concern of ours. He must obey his own conscience. Now, please hurry.

JULIE: But you see, Frau Pastor, it concerns you too.

IDA HALL (*firmly*): Julie, please do as I tell you.

JULIE (*crushed*): I'm sorry, Frau Pastor. (*She goes. Ida comes into the living room, closing the folding doors behind her. She tries to draw the lace curtains over the windows of the folding doors, but abandons the attempt. She looks nervously around the room. Stormtroop Leader* FRITZ GERTE *comes in, abruptly closing the door behind him. He is a man of medium height, about thirty-five years old. His small eyes scan the room suspiciously. He is dressed in S.S. uniform.*)

IDA HALL: Oh, Fritz, how nice to see you.

FRITZ GERTE: Is anyone at home besides you?

IDA HALL: Friedrich is out on parish business and Christine has gone for a walk. Won't you sit?

FRITZ GERTE (*going over to look through the windows in the folding doors*): You're expecting guests, I see.

IDA HALL (*ill at ease*): Only General Grotjahn and his son, Werner.

FRITZ GERTE: The table seems very gaily decorated for such an informal gathering.

IDA HALL: Just a few flowers someone sent from the country.

FRITZ GERTE: On the contrary you bought them at Schmidt's this morning at half-past eleven.

IDA HALL: You seem to be very interested in my movements.

FRITZ GERTE: At the present moment I am particularly interested, Ida.

IDA HALL: Well, since you know so much, is there any need for me to explain?

FRITZ GERTE: I should be interested to hear you try.

IDA HALL: Fritz, you're being very ridiculous. Is there any harm in my entertaining such old friends as the Grotjahns?

FRITZ GERTE: Why did you lie about the flowers?

IDA HALL: I refuse to sit here and be cross-examined by you. If you've something to say why don't you say it? I presume you didn't come here just to insult me.

FRITZ GERTE: I came here for an explanation, but since you refuse to tell me yourself I will tell you. I thought I could trust you, Ida. I thought you were really grateful for all I have tried to do for you, but I see I've been made a fool of and I object to it. Why didn't you tell me that Christine was going to marry Werner von Grotjahn?

IDA HALL: Perhaps, because I didn't want to hurt you. I would have told you later.

FRITZ GERTE: When are they to be married?

IDA HALL: Tomorrow morning at ten o'clock. We are having a little celebration tonight.

FRITZ GERTE: Interesting. When were the banns published?

IDA HALL: The registrar arranged that for us. He is an old friend of General Grotjahn's.

FRITZ GERTE: Very far-seeing of you, Ida. General Grotjahn has quite a band of monarchist traitors who can be relied on to keep their mouths shut.

IDA HALL: The only reason I tried to keep this from you was because I knew you would be upset about it. Werner and Christine have known each other for some time. A few days ago he got an invitation to go to Columbia University in New York. He has to leave at once. Of course, it's a great honor for him.

FRITZ GERTE: A great honor for a German to be invited to an enemy country.

IDA HALL: Hardly that, Fritz. We are not at war with America yet.

FRITZ GERTE: And I suppose the loyal pastor would not have cared for his daughter to marry a member of the National Socialist party? He prefers the son of a man who sneers at our attempts to lead Germany back to the position of honor, which he and his monarchist friends lost for her.

IDA HALL: Friedrich knows nothing about your attachment to Christine and in any case he would never attempt to influence her. Now, please, Fritz, try to look at this matter calmly. I know it has been difficult to invite you to this house as often as I would have liked. Friedrich has been hard to manage these past years and often he says things which are harmful to himself but . . .

FRITZ GERTE: I think, Ida, you'd do better to leave your excuses to my imagination; they sound rather hollow to me. You ask me to look at this matter calmly. Would you, if you had worked as I have to keep your husband's blundering, God-fearing sermons from reaching the ears of the authorities in Berlin? For the past two years I have constantly risked my reputation to help you. I have been made the laughing stock of my comrades and what have you done for me? When have you made one single attempt to show any gratitude?

IDA HALL: Fritz, please.

FRITZ GERTE: Allow me one moment. Perhaps you have forgotten that your husband was an outlaw from society here until I consented to become your protector? Perhaps you have forgotten how I arranged for Christine to present the Leader with a bouquet of flowers and how the Leader was kind enough to kiss her on both cheeks? It certainly looks as if I have been making rather a fool of myself by shielding you and your precious family.

IDA HALL: I have forgotten nothing.

FRITZ GERTE: In that case I am overwhelmed by your gratitude.

IDA HALL: Is your sarcasm really necessary?

FRITZ GERTE: Like everyone else, I'm only human.

IDA HALL: Does this marriage really mean so much to you?

FRITZ GERTE (*quite simply*): I love Christine. (*He walks slowly over to the window. Ida watches him*) She's about the only person I ever cared for.

IDA HALL: I couldn't prevent it, Fritz.

FRITZ GERTE: I've been in love with her since she was a child.

IDA HALL: Christine isn't a child any longer, Fritz. She's as self-willed as her father.

FRITZ GERTE (*breaking out*): What does a girl of eighteen know about life? And you stand there and tell me you couldn't prevent the marriage. Haven't I got everything to offer her—an assured future, a respectable position, a nice home? What more could she have?

IDA HALL: A man whom she loves.

FRITZ GERTE: And I suppose if her choice falls on a man notorious for his lack of loyalty, you can still do nothing to prevent the marriage?

IDA HALL: Fritz, please be quiet. The servants will hear you. Werner has never said anything disloyal.

FRITZ GERTE: Silence is often more disloyal than words.

IDA HALL: I had no right to interfere.

FRITZ GERTE: No right! You're being a little too naïve, my dear Ida. Why not lay your cards on the table?

IDA HALL: I don't understand you.

FRITZ GERTE: Oh, yes, you do. When you begged me for my help to save your huband from the consequences of his wretched sermons, when you went down on your knees to me . . .

IDA HALL: You're talking pure nonsense, Fritz. I never did any such thing.

FRITZ GERTE: But you promised me your daughter's love.

IDA HALL: No. How could I promise you something outside my power to give? I said if Christine loved you, I would be very happy. (*Passionately*) Oh, Fritz, can't you see that this engagement came as a complete surprise? I had hoped and hoped that she would learn to care for you. Do you think it's pleasant for a mother to see her daughter married into a family that's under suspicion? God knows I've tried hard enough to keep my husband from saying the things he does, so that we could enjoy a little peace. I've begged, implored Christine not to do this, but she hasn't listened.

FRITZ GERTE: Naturally, when there's a legacy at stake.

IDA HALL: What do you mean?

FRITZ GERTE (*producing a letter from his pocket*): This. Do you recognize the writing?

IDA HALL: It's the General's.

FRITZ GERTE: Correct. General Grotjahn writes to the executor of a certain restaurant-proprietor in New York by the name of Pegge. Did you know him?

IDA HALL: He was my brother. He died last year.

FRITZ GERTE: Interesting. Well, the General writes a harmless letter to the executor. Too harmless for us, my dear Ida. All about the weather and about Lohengrin. But in the middle of this letter there's a little sentence, one little sentence which could break your neck, my dear Ida.

IDA HALL: Arrest me at once, Fritz. Break my neck, only stop playing cat and mouse with me.

FRITZ GERTE (*laughing pleasantly*): "Could," I said, not "will." Well then, the General asks the executor not to send the inheritance to Germany, but to leave it in America. One ought, he writes, to care for and water the bud of inheritance, so that it may flower, grow and thrive. He thinks us absolutely idiotic. As though we don't understand his stupid way of saying it— with flowers. It's smuggling currency, treason to the country, high treason. . . . Imprisonment for life is the punishment, and, if the Court convicts for dishonorable intent, death by the axe.

IDA HALL: What else is there in the letter?

FRITZ GERTE: If you want to know the whole of it, your name is not mentioned. But don't triumph too soon, my dear. This Herr Pegge was your brother, you are the heiress, you dictated the letter to the General, you wanted to bring the money into safety, you coupled Christine with an American tourist.

IDA HALL: The money doesn't belong to me at all. My brother was mad about Christine. She is the heiress.

FRITZ GERTE: So much the worse. For Christine, I mean. You've brought trouble on her as well.

IDA HALL: Then what shall I do?

FRITZ GERTE: I'll help you once more, this time as well. You're a

German woman, your character is spotlessly clean and you'll be given time to prove it. That's why I tell you now, the marriage is off; give the goose which smells so nice and crisp to the Winter-Relief. The ship will sail, but without Christine.

IDA HALL: And what else?

FRITZ GERTE: Keep quiet. Is the American testator safe?

IDA HALL: He is under oath.

FRITZ GERTE: Then he'll keep quiet. The matter of the legacy will not be mentioned. Christine can keep the money intact. But this time I'm going to strike a bargain with you. Christine is a minor. Your husband will forbid this marriage tonight. I shall ring you up at eight fifteen for your answer. That will give you time to explain matters, when your guests arrive.

IDA HALL: And if I can't do it?

FRITZ GERTE: You can puzzle that out for yourself.

IDA HALL: But you can only arrest me. Friedrich and Christine knew nothing about it and you wouldn't dare touch General Grotjahn.

FRITZ GERTE: I have all the evidence I need to arrest Pastor Hall, if I was unscrupulous enough to use it.

IDA HALL: What do you mean?

FRITZ GERTE: Just concern yourself with your own little problem, Ida, and leave me to look after the rest myself. I'm not a member of the Secret Police for nothing.

IDA HALL: Fritz, you can't leave me in this uncertainty. You've always been a good friend of ours. Your mother was one of Friedrich's most loyal parishioners. . . .

FRITZ GERTE (*stopping her*): Please, Ida, don't start fooling me again. We had all this out before. You should have respected my feelings better the last time.

IDA HALL: If it's Friedrich's sermons, they don't do any harm. He takes God's word too literally—he's not really bad.

(*The door opens and Pastor Hall comes in. A tall man of fifty with an erect carriage. When he speaks his voice is gentle and simple, but not sentimental.*)

FRIEDRICH HALL (*For a moment he doesn't see* GERTE. *He goes straight to his desk looking through the papers on it*): I'm

afraid I'm a little late, my dear. I was delayed with the . . .
(*Sees* GERTE) Oh, I didn't see you, Gerte. How are you?

FRITZ GERTE: Heil Hitler! Herr Pastor.

FRIEDRICH: Please don't get up. Did Ida offer you some refreshment? I'm afraid I don't allow cocktails, but we have some schnapps. . . .

FRITZ GERTE (*interrupting*): My mission is ended, Herr Pastor. I only came to see your wife.

FRIEDRICH HALL: Oh, perhaps I am in the way.

FRITZ GERTE: Not at all, I must be going. You may be interested to hear what she has to say to you. Good night. (*He goes.*)

FRIEDRICH HALL: What does that mean?

IDA HALL: Nothing, dear. I'll explain later. Here's your evening cigar. Sit down and rest, you must be tired.

FRIEDRICH HALL: Thank you. (*He has returned to search among his papers.*) Ida, did you happen to tidy away my mail this morning?

IDA HALL: No, dear.

FRIEDRICH HALL: I've been worrying about it all day. Well, I suppose Julie must have. But it's funny, I left some rather important letters I have been keeping.

IDA HALL (*fearfully*): What were they, Friedrich?

FRIEDRICH HALL: Confidential letters from fathers and mothers, with particulars of how our children are being demoralized by the youth movements. I intended issuing a formal complaint. By the way, Ida, what did Gerte want here? I don't very much care to see you entertaining him.

IDA HALL: He came to see me, Friedrich. I didn't send for him.

FRIEDRICH HALL: I see. Of course, I don't mean to appear uncharitable to the fellow but he really cannot be considered a respectable person to come to a clergyman's house. What did he want?

IDA HALL: Friedrich, sit down and try to be patient with me. I'm in terrible trouble.

FRIEDRICH HALL: Well, my dear, I can only try to help you.

IDA HALL: If only you had told me about those letters in your desk.

I would have seen to it that no one came near them, but now I see what Gerte meant.

FRIEDRICH HALL: You don't mean to say that you gave him my letters?

IDA HALL: Of course not. I don't know how he has got hold of them but I am sure he has.

FRIEDRICH HALL: I suppose he stole them, that would really be the simplest way.

IDA HALL: Gerte is not a thief.

FRIEDRICH HALL: According to the new philosophy stealing private papers does not constitute burglary. He'll probably get a medal and his picture will be in all the papers. The new official-dom seems afraid of the confidence which exists between a shepherd and his flock. When trust rests on loyalty and faith it is dangerous to the State. For my own part, I hope he gets some good out of reading them but I fear for the poor people who write them.

IDA HALL: It's not they who are in danger, but you.

FRIEDRICH HALL: Man did not come into the world to shirk danger, my dear.

IDA HALL: What you preach in the church on Sunday, I have to hush up on Monday. And however much you may dislike that man, you might as well know that it is he who has helped me to do it.

FRIEDRICH HALL: You mean Fritz Gerte? (IDA *nods*) I suppose you'll tell me next that I owe him my life.

IDA HALL: If he hadn't protected us, we'd all be in a concentration camp by now.

FRIEDRICH HALL: At least there would be no shame in that.

IDA HALL: You're not being fair to him, Friedrich. Don't forget the promises you made his mother on her deathbed.

FRIEDRICH HALL: Frau Gerte was a brave, good woman and I did my utmost to lead her son into the paths of righteousness, but the man is a scoundrel and no one knew it better than his poor mother. He squeezed every penny out of her while she lived; when I got him the apprentice job in Samuel Levi's shirt factory he repaid me by idling away his time in various dishonorable pursuits. God knows I persuaded Sam often enough to take him back and all the thanks poor Levi got was to see his business proscribed, his house burnt to the ground and his money appropriated. And now Gerte tells me that Levi can thank his stars he's still alive, living as a beggar in London. If conduct such as his is labelled the 'awakened' convictions of national life, I'd sooner live among African cannibals.

IDA HALL: Why should you as a Christian minister doubt his convictions? Didn't he join the Party at a time when almost the whole country was against the Leader?

FRIEDRICH HALL: I don't care a scrap for his political convictions. It's his human ones that concern me. And, really, Ida, I don't know why you think it necessary to defend him to me in this way.

IDA HALL: Perhaps I would like to see you practice some of the charity you preach.

FRIEDRICH HALL: I do not condemn the man because he is a member of the Party. I have known many young men who joined it through true idealism and who have upheld their faith with courage. Gerte does not belong to such a category. Like too many others he is a National Socialist through fear. Courage depends on being able to feel the logic of your deed. It did not require courage for Gerte to drive women and children into the streets without money or clothing. No, Ida dear, God does not always want us to overlook the faults in our brethren. Sometimes He requires us to condemn injustice and cruelty and when His voice calls us we must not be afraid to make ourselves his instruments.

IDA HALL: Friedrich, Friedrich how am I going to make you understand what I have to say, if you continue in this mood!

FRIEDRICH HALL: I shall try to have patience, my dear.

IDA HALL: You think him a cold-hearted bully. But that's not quite true. He has helped us, Friedrich; he has helped you.

FRIEDRICH HALL: I shall try to believe that, too.

IDA HALL: He is in love with Christine. He came here to say that.

FRIEDRICH HALL: Well?

IDA HALL: He thinks we have betrayed his protection by allowing her to marry Werner.

FRIEDRICH HALL: Christine was to be the reward for his services, is that the story? Does he imagine we barter human souls here?

IDA HALL: He says Christine is too young to know her own mind. He is opposed to the marriage taking place tomorrow.

FRIEDRICH HALL: Gerte may be opposed to the sun's rising tomorrow for all I care. Christine has never made any secret of her dislike of him.

IDA HALL: He has power, Friedrich.

FRIEDRICH HALL: But not enough to prevent the sun from rising or Werner marrying Christine. I fear your valiant defense of Gerte is collapsing.

IDA HALL: I promised him that I would try to arrange for him to see as much as possible of Christine, but your antagonism has always made that difficult. He found out about Christine's legacy in America.

FRIEDRICH HALL: That doesn't give him any power to threaten us.

IDA HALL: He holds all of us in his hands. You, because you take the Ten Commandments literally. Me, because . . . Friedrich . . .

FRIEDRICH HALL: What's all this about? What have you done except make an irresponsible promise? Don't you realize how degraded and small this morbid fear makes you? Ida, you always used to be courageous; you've changed completely in the last two years.

IDA HALL: I sent instructions to my brother's executor not to send the money to Germany, because the money would be taken away from Christine here and she'd get scarcely half the amount in marks.

FRIEDRICH HALL: That was very foolish of you, and also against the law.

IDA HALL: I didn't do it openly, but illegally.

FRIEDRICH HALL: So much the worse. . . . Didn't anyone help you in the matter?

IDA HALL: The General. He wrote a letter to New York for me.

The police are in possession of this letter. I've seen it in the hands of . . .

FRIEDRICH HALL: Fritz Gerte. What have you done, Ida? What, in Heaven's name, does it matter whether Christine is blessed with earthly goods or not? Heaven knows I've fought my whole life long with clean hands. Every Sunday I stand in the pulpit, a voice crying in the wilderness, and I defend the teachings of Christ against the teachings of his opponents. I allow myself to be intimidated neither by their threats nor their promises, yet my own wife stabs me in the back. Now they will have their triumph. Look at Pastor Hall, they'll say, he gives out that he's Christian and all the time he smuggles currency. Ida, Ida, if only it were I that was going to suffer. But the truth will suffer injury too, because I, an alleged criminal, proclaim it. . . . What had Gerte to say to this?

IDA HALL: Christine is a minor. You are her guardian. You should refuse to allow her to marry and leave the country tomorrow.

FRIEDRICH HALL: And if I don't do this?

IDA HALL: Then they'll arrest you or me or Christine, or all of us.

FRIEDRICH HALL: This man of honor has made a false calculation. (*He walks over to the writing desk, takes a letter out of it, sits down and begins to write*)

IDA HALL: Who are you writing to?

FRIEDRICH HALL: To your brother's executor. I forbid him to take instructions from anyone but me. He is to send the inheritance immediately, and by legal means, to Germany.

IDA HALL: Then you're making everything still worse. Gerte won't allow that. He's quite agreed that the money stays in America; what he objects to is Christine marrying Werner.

FRIEDRICH HALL: Now I understand. The honorable Stormtroop Leader is provident. And I've got to become his companion in pushing, creeping and betraying . . .

IDA HALL: But there's no other way. Do you want to throw us all into prison? We need only delay the marriage for a few years, until Christine is old enough to decide for herself. Friedrich, I can't endure the shame of it. At least have pity on me.

FRIEDRICH HALL: No, Ida, here human consideration ends—even to you, my wife. I cannot betray the principles of humanity because some fanatic, gorged with power tries to blackmail me.

IDA HALL: But at least think of Christine. Her life will be ruined too.

FRIEDRICH HALL: Gerte is not such a fool as to arrest Christine. If he did that he'd lose both the heiress and the money. Nor will he arrest you. It would look awkward if both the parents of his intended bride were in jail. If God is willing I shall be chosen.

IDA HALL: But how can that help any of us?

FRIEDRICH HALL: This is no longer a squabble around some petty intrigue. Personalities fade away. You and I and all of us are no longer players in a cheap melodrama—we have become symbols of something bigger and better. The word of God stands naked before intolerance, injustice and hatred. It is the test, Ida, that I knew was coming to me. The fight will begin, I shall not cry: O Lord why hast thou chosen me . . .

IDA HALL: No, you won't cry, but what about us? That doesn't concern you, does it? Friedrich, how can you be such an egoist? When you volunteered in the war, although there was no need for a pastor to do so. When you nearly broke my heart with anxiety, you only thought of yourself and your work. When you came back wounded and said you had erred and that from now on you would preach the gospel of pacifism and soften the hearts of humanity, you had no thought of what I and the child might have to suffer, how we were hated and reviled by all around us. During these last years you have never even considered to what hell you might be leaving your child and your wife —only yourself, yourself, yourself. If that's Christianity, I'd rather be a pagan.

FRIEDRICH HALL (*after a pause*): Perhaps you're right, Ida. I think too much of myself and my soul's salvation. I sometimes ask myself whether a man who seeks the truth and wishes to discover nothing but the truth has the right to marry and have children. Perhaps that is my greatest fault.

IDA HALL: I didn't mean to be unkind, Friedrich. Forgive me.

FRIEDRICH HALL: Of course, dear. You do well to remind me of my duty to you.

IDA HALL: Why don't you at least ask Christine and allow her to decide?

FRIEDRICH HALL: I'll do that. (*Julie comes in.*)

JULIE: The shoemaker, Traugott Pipermann, would like a word with you, Herr Pastor. He says he won't delay you more than a few minutes.

FRIEDRICH HALL: Very well, ask him to come in. (JULIE *goes.*)

IDA HALL: I don't think I could stand Pipermann at the moment. Don't let him keep you too long, dear.

FRIEDRICH HALL: I'll do my best. It's never very easy to get rid of Pipermann or to discover what he has come to say for that matter.

IDA HALL: I'll just go and see how dinner is getting along.

(IDA HALL *goes out, rear.* TRAUGOTT PIPERMANN *comes in, an elderly man whose leanness gives the impression of wrinkledness and dryness. He has a small goat's beard, which covers his receding chin. He wears nickel spectacles with blue glasses on his pointed nose. He has the habit of taking off his spectacles and putting them on again. When he takes them off, one sees small, restless eyes, which he keeps lowered when he speaks. The small mouth is drooping and, when he is not speaking, rounded like the head of a nail. He is wearing a second-hand, old-fashioned suit with a waistcoat buttoned up to the neck.*)

FRIEDRICH HALL (*shakes Pipermann's hand*): Well, my dear Pipermann, to what do I owe the honor of this visit?

TRAUGOTT PIPERMANN: Although it's no honor for you, Herr Pastor, yet it's a pleasure for me to see you in good health.

FRIEDRICH HALL: Sit down. What can I offer you? A schnapps?

(TRAUGOTT PIPERMANN *and* FRIEDRICH HALL *sit down*)

TRAUGOTT PIPERMANN: Although it's no sin, and the Holy Scriptures only forbid debauchery, yet I prefer to renounce alcohol.

FRIEDRICH HALL: Of course, of course, fancy my not thinking of it! You're a teetotaller.

TRAUGOTT PIPERMANN: Your question took me aback, Herr Pastor, because the Innkeeper Henke also wanted to tempt me when I was collecting the church dues from him, and the Innkeeper Henke is badly disposed towards me, that is, badly disposed towards you, I meant to say, Herr Pastor, yet I believe you when you say you did it out of absentmindedness.

FRIEDRICH HALL: My dear Pipermann, Herr Henke likes to play a practical joke now and then.

TRAUGOTT PIPERMANN: The devil comes among us in many forms, Herr Pastor.

FRIEDRICH HALL: As you rightly observe, Pipermann, the devil comes among us in many forms. And now what exactly have you come here for?

TRAUGOTT PIPERMANN: Although as a skilled shoemaker I know how to distinguish a sole made of the best leather from one made of the bits that are left over, Herr Pastor, yet I think that if I had no other choice, and couldn't get the best leather sole, I'd resort to one made of the bits that are left over and rely on the good God for it to stand the wear and tear.

FRIEDRICH HALL: Naturally.

TRAUGOTT PIPERMANN (*rubbing his hands together*): I'm delighted, Herr Pastor, I can't tell you how glad I am. (FRIEDRICH HALL *doesn't follow, but since he knows him and his circumlocutory prologues when he has some proposition to make, for which he only has half the necessary courage, he becomes attentive*) Although I believe myself, in all humility, to be a good Christian, and the seventh day is a veritable day of God to me, and I'd sooner eat dry bread than hand round beer and schnapps of a Sunday, yet we all owe obedience to the State, and I have to protect myself against the rain with a mackintosh and goloshes, otherwise I get wet, and when facts are against us we can't always be running against the facts, yet, before it's too late, we have to seal our lips and hold the Word in our hearts. God will see it there, even if we don't show it to the world, which dwells in sin and goes along crooked paths. Otherwise, our deeds can easily be interpreted as pride and arrogance, and where pride has entry, there the Tempter becomes a guest.

FRIEDRICH HALL: We talk in parables, Pipermann, but it would be as well to understand each other. You have come here to deliver a message—if I may try to interpret that message it is this. You would have me abandon my work here, lest we incur the anger of certain gentlemen, who object to hearing the truth. We must not hide our light under a bushel, my dear Pipermann. That also is a parable. Stop me if I misinterpret you.

PIPERMANN: Although I do not want to contradict your great learning, dear Pastor, yet I would not wish others to interpret my words in such a way.

FRIEDRICH HALL: Be that as it may. And now am I to understand you are speaking as a private individual or with a mandate from the parish, that's to say, as Churchwarden?

TRAUGOTT PIPERMANN: Although I'm talking as a humble, private individual, yet a great many members of the parish think as I do; even the Innkeeper Henke, in whose favor, may God have mercy on him, it would be difficult for me to find anything else to say. Everyone agrees things can't go on like this. Something is bound to happen.

FRIEDRICH HALL: Things can't go on like what? What's bound to happen?

TRAUGOTT PIPERMANN: The State assistance will be withdrawn from us, and the church roof is dilapidated and in danger of falling in, if we don't re-sole, repair it, I meant to say, and also they'll stop the stipendiary of the parish. People—especially Innkeeper Henke, are saying, and the Nazis even threaten to boycott our businesses, yet threats and persecution shouldn't disturb us. The Pharisees didn't spare our Lord even from death on the Cross, only I mean to say, we ought . . . we ought . . . (*He stutters and, confused, doesn't know how to finish.*)

FRIEDRICH HALL (*without relenting, leaves him for some seconds in his confusion*): You mean to say that first of all we should think of the church roof, and only then of the church's foundations. When a customer comes to you and entrusts you with the task of making a pair of shoes, you take his measure, as I know from my own experience, conscientiously, and you provide him with shoes, which don't pinch and cause him to have corns, shoes which fit well and suit his feet. How the shoes are em-

bellished, whether with a row of perforated holes or with flat
toes, you think, quite rightly, is of secondary importance.
What's the use of an elegant, fashionable shoe, if the customer
can't walk and groans with pain? Do you follow me? The
church roof is a sign of respect, but first of all come the foundations. That is something which I will discuss with no one, except my own conscience. If a customer is dissatisfied with you,
he goes to another shoemaker. I'll raise the matter at the next
sitting of the parish council and put it to a vote of confidence.

TRAUGOTT PIPERMANN: In Heaven's name, Herr Pastor. Although
I underlined the fact that I came here as a private individual,
and had only your own good in view, yet you've misunderstood
me. Not many folk in the parish would come to you as a gen-
uine friend, or follow you through thick and thin when the
worst comes to the worst. Although that's another question,
concerning which I wouldn't allow myself to offer an opinion.

FRIEDRICH HALL: I thank you, I thank you, my dear Pipermann,
I know how to value your friendship. A weight has fallen from
my heart. I need the trust of the parish; at this very moment I
need it more than ever before.

TRAUGOTT PIPERMANN: You can count on me, Herr Pastor, although
there are many things I'd like to talk over with you, things of
a worldly nature. It seems that the son of the shopkeeper
Wrede has ensnared the bar maid of the Innkeeper Henke and
has even tried to force himself into her bedroom at night. Yet
my time is measured and perhaps yours is also—(TRAUGOTT
PIPERMANN *ought to stand up at this point, yet he waits for
Friedrich Hall to invite him to stay, so for that reason he doesn't
get out of his chair*)

FRIEDRICH HALL (*stands up, thus compelling* PIPERMANN *to get up
as well*): Unfortunately, my dear Pipermann. We'll meet again
very soon, I hope, then we'll talk over the worldly matters. Not
as Pharisees, like those scandal-mongers, who are as insufferable
to you as they are to me, but with one serene and with one
damp eye, as is seemly for men who know life as it is. (TRAU-
GOTT PIPERMANN *takes his leave, flattered, and goes out of the
room with a great deal of bowing*)

FRIEDRICH HALL: Ouff! (*He goes to the window and opens it. Presently* IDA HALL *comes in from the rear door.*)

IDA HALL: Has he gone?

FRIEDRICH HALL: At last.

IDA HALL: What did he want this time?

FRIEDRICH HALL: Parish affairs. He thinks we won't get a new roof for the church unless we adopt a more humble attitude toward the state.

IDA HALL: Why doesn't he start a fund for its repair? He's rich enough. (*A knock*)

FRIEDRICH HALL: Come in, Traugott Pipermann. (PIPERMANN *comes back*)

TRAUGOTT PIPERMANN: Excuse me, Herr Pastor. Although I had already gone, yet I forgot my spectacles.

FRIEDRICH HALL: Your spectacles? Here you are. (*Hands them to him*)

TRAUGOTT PIPERMANN: A thousand thanks. (*Puts them on.*) Gracious lady, my humblest respects. (*He bows himself out backwards.*) I apologize for interrupting your honorable discourse.

IDA HALL: What he doesn't see behind those blue spectacles of his, isn't worth recording. No girl is safe from his shameless glances.

FRIEDRICH HALL (*smiling*): You mustn't take him so seriously, Ida. "Although" his glances are shameless, "yet" his heart is bashful and no one can accuse him of a "worldly" deed. (JULIE *comes in.*)

JULIE: Herr General von Grotjahn. (*To Ida Hall*) Didn't you want to dress, Frau Pastor? (JULIE *goes out. Enter* GENERAL VON GROTJAHN *in black frock coat and striped trousers, a monocle in his eye. He is about sixty years old, rather round and comfortable.*)

PAUL VON GROTJAHN (*he goes across to Ida Hall and kisses her hand*): My dear Ida, you look as if it were you who was the bride. (*Shakes Friedrich Hall by the hand*) She's radiant as a rose in May, isn't she, my dear Friedrich?

> "T'was in the wondrous month of May
> When all the buds did spring

That in my heart
Love first began to sing."
Poet unknown, as the new saying goes.

FRIEDRICH HALL: Wrong, Paul. The poem is by Goethe, not Heine.

PAUL VON GROTJAHN: Goethe wasn't quite house-broken either, you know. First place he was a Freemason, and second too much of a cosmopolitan.

FRIEDRICH HALL: Will you have a schnapps?

PAUL VON GROTJAHN: Did you ever know me to refuse? Ah! Your daughter's marrying the son of an old drunkard. Here's luck! Bad habit, Ida, bad habit. Still the regiment, you know, everyone does.

IDA HALL: Well, you've had a gay life, Paul.

PAUL VON GROTJAHN: Damn it, you're right, Ida, you're right. One of the old brigade. Damn few of us left. Can't gag my mouth though, just like to see them try. But I'm quite harmless really, except of course in 1918, before Verdun. Colonel von Grotjahn, then, I remember as well, as I remember yesterday. . . .

IDA HALL: If you won't think me very rude, Paul, I must go and change.

PAUL VON GROTJAHN: Want to make yourself still more beautiful, eh?

IDA HALL: I've been helping cook with the dinner. (*She goes.*)

FRIEDRICH HALL: Help yourself to another schnapps, Paul. I have something to say to you.

PAUL VON GROTJAHN: Never say no. Damn it, what was I saying? Oh, yes, before Verdun. Of course, you weren't there, didn't agree with the war, what? Pacifist, weren't you. Damned silly business. Shouldn't have done that, old fellow.

FRIEDRICH HALL: I saw enough of it to persuade me it was wrong.

PAUL VON GROTJAHN: Must do something to make men of us. Here's health!

FRIEDRICH HALL: Paul, I want to have a few words with you about this marriage.

PAUL VON GROTJAHN: Too ceremonious, Friedrich. Say things bluntly—that's the soldier's way. Remember as well as I remem-

ber yesterday when I was a red-nosed Cadet. Color-sergeant
Siebenklotz said to me, Grotjahn you believe in the stork? At
your service, no, I said. Then forward, on top of the enemy,
says he and gives me the address of a first class Venus. First one
I had, nice little piece. Short in the leg you know, couldn't sit
a horse. Siebenklotz, a fine fellow killed next year.

FRIEDRICH HALL (*smiling reproachfully*): Paul!

PAUL VON GROTJAHN: Stupid of me. Forgot. . . . Clergymen, of
course, don't like talking about it.

FRIEDRICH HALL: You wrote a letter to my brother-in-law's executor
telling him not to send Christine's inheritance over to Germany.

PAUL VON GROTJAHN: That comes of doing anything for women.
Can't keep their mouths shut.

FRIEDRICH HALL: Do you realize that it's against the law?

PAUL VON GROTJAHN: Too many laws. Anyway I'm not having
laws dictated to me by an ex-corporal. Bad discipline.

FRIEDRICH HALL: It isn't any business of ours to pass judgment on
the merits or demerits of the laws.

PAUL VON GROTJAHN: Obey and keep our mouths shut, eh? That
would suit the fellows pretty well. Then they'd have us just
where they want us. But we haven't sunk as low as that not by a
long chalk. You should try listening to what the people say on
the street. They knuckle under, but they know exactly what's
up. Today I was at the newspaper stall, turning over the papers.
The shopkeeper has put the *Voelkischer Beobachter* on top to
let everyone know he is a Nazi. Said he, Herr General, why do
you take so long choosing, they're twelve to the dozen, the lies
are printed in black and the truths in white so that no one can
read them.

FRIEDRICH HALL: The letter which you wrote to the American lawyer is now in the hands of the Secret Police.

PAUL VON GROTJAHN: Damn it all! Then I'm in a pickle already.

FRIEDRICH HALL: Does it all still seem a joke to you?

PAUL VON GROTJAHN: What can they prove against me? I'll talk my
way out of it. Friends at the ministry, you know.

FRIEDRICH HALL: Yes, but I happen to be a nuisance to them. Now,
at last they have found a weapon to destroy me.

PAUL VON GROTJAHN: Friedrich, I'm a fool . . . I'm an old ass . . . Should have thought of that before. What'll happen now?

FRIEDRICH HALL: It's not your faul, Paul. I don't blame you.

PAUL VON GROTJAHN: Damned sorry, old fellow. Anything I can do. . . . (*Enter* CHRISTINE HALL *and* WERNER VON GROTJAHN. CHRISTINE HALL *is eighteen years old, pretty face, gentle ways, a gay manner.* WERNER VON GROTJAHN *is stiff in walking, dry, but not lacking in temperament. He is twenty-six years old*.)

PAUL VON GROTJAHN (*to* CHRISTINE): Don't I get a kiss, my lovely little daughter? (CHRISTINE HALL *kisses the* GENERAL.) Where have you two come from?

WERNER VON GROTJAHN: Straight from the airport. We've been booking the seats.

CHRISTINE HALL: The plane leaves at twelve and we'll be in London at four. Won't be much time for the wedding breakfast.

WERNER VON GROTJAHN: Unless we ask your father to cut the service down.

PAUL VON GROTJAHN: Good idea. Don't like too much pow-wow from the pulpit. Sorry, Friedrich, nothing personal.

FRIEDRICH HALL: Certainly, Paul, you never were much of a hand at hearing other people talk. Now, if you will excuse me a minute I'll tell Ida we're all here.

PAUL VON GROTJAHN: Too much family, what? (FRIEDRICH HALL *goes*). Didn't you drop into town on the way back?

CHRISTINE HALL: Yes, we stopped at Waag's for coffee, the last time we'll go there for years. Werner and I had a bit of a quarrel.

PAUL VON GROTJAHN: Good sign. Always quarrel on your wedding eve. Brings luck. What was the row about?

WERNER VON GROTJAHN: Christine wanted to know what I thought a man ought to do if he knew the sun would grow cold tomorrow.

PAUL VON GROTJAHN: Get drunk, of course.

CHRISTINE: I said he should be very nice to his wife, but Werner said that as an astronomer he would have to note down what was happening on the earth as long as he could for the benefit of any future forms of life.

PAUL VON GROTJAHN: Comes of meddling with stars. Damn silly

subject. Always told his mother he ought to go in the army.

WERNER VON GROTJAHN: Anyway we made it up, didn't we, Christine?

CHRISTINE HALL: Yes. Look what a lovely bracelet Werner bought me. (*Shows it to* GENERAL GROTJAHN.)

PAUL VON GROTJAHN: Been bribing you, eh?

CHRISTINE HALL: I like being bribed. Werner, when we're married, you must still go shopping with me and buy me presents, but you mustn't say we're married.

WERNER VON GROTJAHN: What am I to say?

CHRISTINE HALL: What did you say, papa?

PAUL VON GROTJAHN: Me? Don't remember.

CHRISTINE HALL: Yes, you do. You said your wife was your unmarried cousin and that you had to pay for her because she couldn't get a husband.

PAUL VON GROTJAHN (*laughing*): Cute little minx! I believe I did. All the same I was damned faithful. A paragon of fidelity. The most faithful man on God's earth.

CHRISTINE HALL: I don't believe you. (FRIEDRICH HALL *and* IDA HALL *come in. Ida has changed into evening dress*): Mother, darling, you ought to have heard the General lying. He says he was a paragon of virtue.

IDA HALL (*not heeding her*): Yes, dear.

CHRISTINE HALL (*noticing her mother's preoccupation*): What's the matter? You both look so serious.

FRIEDRICH HALL: Christine, darling, before we go in to supper I have something to say to you. It concerns you all.

WERNER VON GROTJAHN (*moving to Christine*): Has something happened?

FRIEDRICH HALL: We must try to be calm and serious. I have been told to forbid your marriage.

WERNER VON GROTJAHN: On what grounds? Who demanded that?

IDA HALL (*unable to control her agitation*): Werner, my dear, it's Stormtroop Leader Gerte. He doesn't want Christine to go away. He—(*she can't finish.*)

WERNER VON GROTJAHN: He wants her himself, is that the story?

IDA HALL: He doesn't want her to marry you.

WERNER VON GROTJAHN: But he can't stop it. What have I done? What has he against me?

PAUL VON GROTJAHN: That you use a civilized form of greeting instead of extending your arm like a crane and yelling, "Heil, Hitler."

CHRISTINE HALL: But, mother, they can't do this, they can't. I love Werner. We're going to be married. Papa, you won't do it will you? Will you? (*She goes to Friedrich Hall and buries her head against his chest.*)

FRIEDRICH HALL: I wan't to do the best for us all, my treasure.

WERNER VON GROTJAHN: But this is fantastic. I've never spoken a word against the Leader.

PAUL VON GROTJAHN: Probably, it's because you're your father's son. The sins of the fathers shall be visited upon the children . . . can't remember the rest of it. Anyhow, that's the only thing they've learnt from the Jews.

WERNER VON GROTJAHN: But, Pastor Hall, you're not going to forbid our marriage now? You're not really thinking of it, are you?

IDA HALL: He must, Werner. Don't you see what will . . .

FRIEDRICH HALL (*interrupting her*): One moment, Ida. Werner and Christine, are you prepared to accept all the consequences of this marriage?

WERNER VON GROTJAHN: But they can't touch us, can they? And even if they do, I'll risk it. What do you say, Christine?

CHRISTINE HALL: I don't care what happens to me. I won't fall into the hands of Fritz Gerte. I couldn't bear that.

WERNER VON GROTJAHN: Even if we are never allowed to come back to Germany, even that would be better.

IDA HALL: No, no it's not that. It's not you who will suffer, it's . . .

FRIEDRICH HALL (*firmly*): Quiet, Ida.

CHRISTINE HALL (*suddenly realizing*): You mean, it's you. They'll arrest you. . . . (*Pause.*) Papa, darling, they won't arrest you, will they?

FRIEDRICH HALL (*his eyes fixed on Ida, implying her silence*): No.

WERNER VON GROTJAHN: Then we'll run the risk, won't we, Christine? I know it's hard on you two and father. But we'll be safe and happy in America. I've so much to look forward to there.

CHRISTINE HALL: And we'll write to you often and you'll all come over and see us one day.

FRIEDRICH HALL: You'll be happy. Now, let us go and eat our supper. Come, Ida, you lead the way.

CHRISTINE HALL: And we'll all be cheerful and happy as if nothing was going to happen.

FRIEDRICH HALL: Just as if nothing was going to happen. Go on, dear. (*Ida, Christine and Werner open the folding doors and go into the dining room. General von Grotjahn goes to Friedrich Hall.*)

PAUL VON GROTJAHN: Brave fellow, Friedrich. Couldn't have been much of a pacifist about you in the war.

FRIEDRICH HALL: Come along. (*Friedrich Hall and Paul von Grotjahn follow the others. All stay standing before their places.*) Our father, that art in Heaven, hallowed be thy name. Thy kingdom come, thy will be done, on earth as it is in Heaven. Give us this day our daily bread and forgive us our trespasses, as we forgive them that trespass against us. Lead us not into temptation but deliver us from evil, for thine is the kingdom, the power and the glory. For ever and ever. Amen.

ALL: Amen. (*Ida Hall signs to them to sit. Julie brings in the roast beef. Pastor Hall stands up to carve.*)

PAUL VON GROTJAHN: Ah, roast beef, nothing like it, unless it be bully-beef. Had too much of that in the army, never been the same since.

CHRISTINE HALL: What did it do to you, Papa?

PAUL VON GROTJAHN: Rumbles, my dear, rumbles.

WERNER VON GROTJAHN: Father!

FRIEDRICH HALL: No, Werner, we'll allow Paul to say exactly what he likes tonight. We won't be shocked.

PAUL VON GROTJAHN: Then you'll not get a whistle out of me. Prim as a Puritan. Where's the use, if no one is shocked?

WERNER VON GROTJAHN: You're not eating anything, Frau Hall.

IDA HALL (*rousing herself*): I? Oh, it's just that I was disappointed no one has noticed my flowers and I ordered them specially.

WERNER VON GROTJAHN: They're wonderful.

PAUL VON GROTJAHN: Wonderful! Takes a woman to think of everything. . . . Would you mind passing the salt, Friedrich?

IDA HALL: Isn't the beef salt enough, Paul? I took such care not to overdo it. I remembered your complaint last time.

CHRISTINE HALL: He wants his bully-beef after all. Rumbles, I think I'll call you that in future.

PAUL VON GROTJAHN: Well, talking of internal complaints are you afraid of air-sickness tomorrow?

CHRISTINE HALL: Not in the least.

IDA HALL: My knees begin to tremble even on a river steamer.

WERNER VON GROTJAHN: We'll telegraph as soon as we land in New York, won't we, Christine?

CHRISTINE HALL: It's going to be heavenly, five days of nothing but water·and wind and clouds.

FRIEDRICH HALL: Christine, what will you miss most in our old house? The old beech in the garden?

CHRISTINE HALL: Yes, that certainly.

FRIEDRICH HALL: Do you still remember how when you were a child you used to climb to the top and hide yourself in the leaves?

IDA HALL: She wouldn't come down. One day, Friedrich asked her: What do you see when you're up there?

PAUL VON GROTJAHN: And what did she see?

FRIEDRICH HALL: God playing hide and seek with the clouds. . . . But you haven't yet told me what you'll miss most of all?

CHRISTINE HALL: Our old musical clock.

FRIEDRICH HALL: I had it from my father, and he inherited it from his father.

CHRISTINE HALL: It's so old now that it plays only when it wants to. It stops suddenly and then, after a while, begins to play again. (*The telephone rings.* IDA HALL *jumps up.*)

JULIE: I'll go and answer it.
(JULIE *goes out*)

IDA HALL: If it's for me, call me at once.

FRIEDRICH HALL: Who'd ring up so late, Ida?

IDA HALL: How late is it?

WERNER VON GROTJAHN: Exactly quarter past eight. (IDA HALL *sighs*) Aren't you well, Mama?

IDA HALL: I'm as fit as a fiddle.

PAUL VON GROTJAHN: Of course, a young woman like you!

IDA HALL: I don't make any claim to being young any longer, at any rate not after today. . . . The mother of a married daughter.

(JULIE *comes in*)

JULIE: It was the travel bureau. The car from the flying field will be here punctually at eleven o'clock.

PAUL VON GROTJAHN: What does the musical clock play . . . when it plays, that is?

CHRISTINE HALL: "The God who planted iron here
          Wanted no man as slave."

PAUL VON GROTJAHN: Damned good! A musical clock that plays high treason!

CHRISTINE HALL: During the last few years, mother hasn't let us turn it on, on account of the servants.

FRIEDRICH HALL (*quickly, coming to the protection of his wife*): It grates and groans so pitifully when it's in a sulky mood that it's really no pleasure to play it any longer.

CHRISTINE HALL: May I wind it up today? Who knows when I'll hear it again?

FRIEDRICH HALL: Of course you may. (CHRISTINE HALL *stands up, goes to the musical clock and winds it up. It gives out a grating and groaning. Then silence*) You see what it's like.

PAUL VON GROTJAHN (*laughing*): Even the musical clock is afraid of being denounced. It refuses to sing a song in which the word "freedom" occurs.

FRIEDRICH HALL: Our rulers speak also of freedom. One has to invent new ideas; the dictators have stolen the old ones and brought them within their own sense.

WERNER VON GROTJAHN: Today I am free because others are afraid of me.

FRIEDRICH HALL: That's it. Freedom means making the other nations afraid of us.

CHRISTINE HALL: Oh, do stop talking about politics. Is there nothing more beautiful than stupid politics? You're always wrangling over words and each of you means something different. I don't know any longer what you all mean.

WERNER VON GROTJAHN (*pedantic*): Words exist in order that people may understand one another.

CHRISTINE HALL: My feelings tell me what's good and what's bad.

WERNER VON GROTJAHN: Feelings too can be reckoned. One can add them and subtract them and reduce them to a common denominator.

CHRISTINE HALL (*laughing*): Don't make a mistake in your reckonings, Werner.

(JULIE *brings in the dessert*)

IDA HALL: Julie, the champagne.

(JULIE *brings the champagne, pours it out. The musical clock suddenly begins to play. While it is playing,* Paul von Grotjahn *speaks the words, with pathos*)

THE SONG:

The God who planted iron here
Wanted no man as slave.
Thus, to man, sabre, sword and spear,
To guard his rights he gave.
Then gave him too his fearless mood,
The wrath of the free word,
That he might uphold till his blood
And till his death, the feud.

So thus we will what God has willed,
Our righteous trust to hold,
Never to let men's skulls be spilled
Before a tyrant's gold.
But who for toys and shame does fight
We hew to little pieces,
In German lands he'll have no right
No German heritage be his.

FRIEDRICH HALL: This glass, my dear Julie, is for you, and you must be with us when we drink to the health and happiness of the young couple.

JULIE (*confused*): Oh, Herr Pastor. . . .

FRIEDRICH HALL: Who has more right than you, my dear Julie, who have faithfully served in our house for nineteen years, to be with us in this festive hour. Please sit down with us.

(JULIE *looks uncomprehendingly for a moment at the Pastor, then gulps and runs out quickly*)

IDA HALL: Let her go. She's very upset at Christine's going away.

CHRISTINE HALL: Poor Julie. I shall miss her.

FRIEDRICH HALL (*rising*): And now, Christine, I'm going to make a little speech in your honor. Perhaps both you and Werner will forgive me if I seem to be a little bit of the clergyman as well. But it's the last sermon you'll hear. After Paul's remarks about pulpit oratory, I've decided to cut the sermon out of our little marriage service tomorrow.

PAUL VON GROTJAHN: Didn't mean it, Friedrich, old man. Stick in the sermon again. Good discipline to try and stop ourselves from going to sleep.

FRIEDRICH HALL: No, we'll have the sermon with the dinner and if you don't like it you can bury your heads in your plates. My dear children I want above all things that you should be happy. I pray God to give you his wisdom and teach you to love each other always. I will try to give you my own answer to the question of how so you may mutually love and understand one another. I know that people don't ask this question any longer, in fact they ask no more questions. Questions are not suited to these times. But we, however, want to ask questions because all earthly things are questionable, because questioning is becoming conscious of oneself, and it clarifies and strengthens this necessity: we recognize as a command which we voluntarily submit to, we test the convention by its worth to us and our time. We need strength for the question and courage for the answer. Many are those who shirk the question, many those who break the answer to pieces. . . . Two human beings who love each other are a world, not hatred nor calumny nor power can shake them, moreover, no temp-

tation, no mood, no wrong path of emotion can darken their
lives. True marriage is joy and fulfillment given as a task and
as a present. Does this mean fleeing from responsibility, from
the duties and burdens of the time, shutting the doors and
hanging curtains over the windows against what is outside?
No. It means: living in the Brotherhood of God, in which all
men are equal, and all needing love and salvation; showing
faith, honesty and an open heart; inspiring confidence and
being worthy of confidence; and rejoicing in the meadows and
shadows of the clouds, the animals and flowers, and the light
of day. We drink to your health, dear daughter, dear son.

*(At the beginning of this speech, the telephone has begun to
ring, shortly at first, then long and angrily. At the first tinkle
IDA HALL would like to jump up and go outside. When FRIED-
RICH HALL looks searchingly at her, she sits down again. When
the telephone rings again she stiffens, her eyes are unblinking.
FRIEDRICH HALL raises his glass. All stand up and drink. At this
moment the musical clock begins to play. Heavy knocks on the
door outside. The door is forced open. Two officers of the
Gestapo in uniform come in. One of them levels a revolver at
the company. Another, with handcuffs in his hand, remains
standing at the door of the dining room and looks around as
if searching for someone)*

FIRST OFFICER: Which of you is Pastor Friedrich Hall? (FRIED-
RICH HALL *pushes his chair away and slowly approaches him*)
By order of the Secret Police!

FRIEDRICH HALL: May God be praised.

FIRST OFFICER: You'll soon drop your high and mighty ways!

FRIEDRICH HALL: Amen.

*(They lead the Pastor out. Nobody at the supper table moves.
They stand there frozen by the shock. The musical clock goes
on playing and then slowly runs down, ending with a wheezing
grunt. Julie runs in, throwing herself on her knees before Ida
Hall.)*

JULIE: Blessed Jesus, what have I done. . . . He said my hair
would be cut off like the girls who've walked out with Jews, if
I didn't tell him where the letters were. . . . Spit on me, frau

Pastor, I can't bear it any longer. I'll throw myself in the river.

IDA HALL: It's all right, Julie. You'll stay here with us, just as before.

Curtain

ACT TWO

ACT TWO

Two weeks later.
Concentration Camp.
The central square of the Concentration Camp. Around the
sides there is a suggestion of the barrack buildings. At the back
stands the central gate of the prison camp above which is a
machine-gun tower with the threatening machine-gun in a
roofed-in room. Right and left of the gate is a high wooden
fence with barbed wire. Behind this sentries are seen marching
past.
In the center of the square a small group of prisoners standing
in two lines. These are Barrack Seven. They stand to attention.
The prisoners' heads are drooped. They wear gray-flecked drill-
trousers and drill-jackets, caps without peaks and heavy laced
boots; on their chests and backs, prison signs. Political prisoners
wear long, red rectangular stripes sewn on the left side of the
chest and on the back of the jacket. Ordinary criminals wear
green bands on the lower sleeve and trousers. Jews are identified
by corresponding green bands over which a yellow circle of
cotton, covering the stripes, is sewn. Emigrants wear similar
cotton circles of a blue color.
EGON FREUNDLICH, *foreman of Barrack Seven, stands in front of*
his squad. He is a powerfully built man.
EGON FREUNDLICH: Barrack Seven. . . . Right dress! (FREUNDLICH
goes to one end of the first line.)
(*The Prisoners have now turned their eyes to the right and shuf-*
fle into position. Another prisoner in the right of the second
rank has stepped to a position parallel with FREUNDLICH *and*
proceeds to dress the rear rank.)
EGON FREUNDLICH: Number two, pull your belly in. . . . Number
five, half a pace to your rear . . . (*This latter order is delivered*

to FRIEDRICH HALL, *who makes no attempt to obey.*) Hey, there, number five, wake up! (*Still Friedrich Hall remains motionless.* EGON FREUNDLICH *walks over to him.*) Here, you, are you deaf? (*He pushes* FRIEDRICH HALL *back.*)

FRIEDRICH HALL: I'm sorry, I didn't know you were addressing me.

EGON FREUNDLICH: Well, you know now. Perhaps you'll be so kind as to draw back your right shoulder and place your hand along the seam of your trousers. We don't stand for any individuality here, you know.

AUGUST KARSCH (*a largely-built fellow with the hands of a laborer*): Here, Freundlich, put him in the rear rank. He'll spoil the whole damned squad.

EGON FREUNDLICH: Shut your dirty mug!

AUGUST KARSCH: I don't want to be kept here all night and that's what'll happen if the Commandant comes along and sees any mixup.

EGON FREUNDLICH: Were you put in charge of this squad or was I? Supposing you wait 'till someone asks you to speak.
(*He goes to the front of his squad and addresses them.*) Barrack Seven. . . . Eyes front! . . . By the right——Number!
(*The prisoners number from right to left, the rear rank following on after the front rank have finished.*)

A PRISONER (*at the end of the rear rank*): Twelve. . . . Squad complete, Foreman.

EGON FREUNDLICH: Stand at ease! . . . Stand easy! (*The prisoners relax slightly.*) New arrivals, come over here. (*He takes notebook and pencil from his pocket.*)
(FRIEDRICH HALL *and a second prisoner,* ERWIN KOHN, *step up to* EGON FREUNDLICH. KOHN *is a young man of about nineteen. He is pale and nervous.*)

EGON FREUNDLICH (*to* KOHN): What's your name?

ERWIN KOHN: Erwin Kohn, sir.

EGON FREUNDLICH (*spelling it out*): C. O. H. N. A beautiful and rare name. (*The prisoners laugh.*)

ERWIN KOHN: I spell it with a K, sir. I've been baptized. I mean I'm a Christian.

EGON FREUNDLICH: One of the nobility, eh? Emigrant aren't you?

ERWIN KOHN: Yes, sir.

EGON FREUNDLICH: Why were you such a damned fool to come back to Germany? Didn't the Paris ladies in their undies please you?

ERWIN KOHN: I've never been involved in politics.

EGON FREUNDLICH: Well, what's that got to do with it? You can't get away with a name like yours, you know.

ERWIN KOHN: I didn't like France. I've never been out of Germany before.

EGON FREUNDLICH: Someone ought to have put a bullet in your home-sick heart in the first place. The bloody idiot goes and comes back to the fatherland, where he knows nobody wants him. What did you think would happen to you?

ERWIN KOHN: That I'd be allowed to live.

EGON FREUNDLICH: Lucky for you, if they allow you to die. . . .A living witness of Jewish cowardice, is that what you'd like to be? Christ Almighty, the little sucker is beginning to cry.

ERWIN KOHN: I'm not crying. I'm laughing.

EGON FREUNDLICH: Before long you'll have laughed yourself to death. What's your profession?

ERWIN KOHN: Painter.

EGON FREUNDLICH: House painter?

ERWIN KOHN: No. I was studying in Paris to be an artist. I paint heads.

EGON FREUNDLICH: Heads will roll, Adolf Hitler said. He's quite right too—but they roll into coffins not picture-frames. Rejoin the ranks. (ERWIN KOHN *steps back into line.*)

AUGUST KARSCH: Christ, I feel bloody hungry too. Hurry up, Freundlich, with these damned names.

EGON FREUNDLICH: Shut up or I'll keep you here all night. (*To* FRIEDRICH HALL.) What's your name?

FRIEDRICH HALL: Friedrich Hall.

EGON FREUNDLICH: Profession?

FRIEDRICH HALL: Pastor.

EGON FREUNDLICH: You'll soon get out of that here. You've been up to tricks with your parish flock, eh?

(FRIEDRICH HALL *remains silent*)

EGON FREUNDLICH: You expect me to handle you with kid gloves, because you got a degree at a university, and with politeness, because you know the Lord's Prayer by heart. But there isn't any calling on Jesus and the Apostles here. Praying, telling fortunes by cards and tea-leaves are all right for toothless old women, but not for men schooled to National Socialism. You watch your step. Whoever quotes a word from the Bible here, openly or in secret, receives twenty-five lashes, like Herder. Fall in.

(*Looks round impatiently*)

Where the hell has that new camp commandant gone to? (*He walks to one side and fills in the entries of the new prisoners in his notebook.*)

AUGUST KARSCH: He's a bit scared of the new commandant.

HERMANN STETLER (*a fat merchant*): Why? He can't be any worse than the last.

AUGUST KARSCH: Afraid he'll lose his job. The old commandant only appointed criminals as foremen.

HERMANN STETLER: Well?

AUGUST KARSCH: Can't say what the new one will do. Might have some of the young stormtroopers sent up; try their hand out or something.

ERWIN KOHN: Was Freundlich a criminal?

AUGUST KARSCH: Yep! He's doing five years for raping children.

EGON FREUNDLICH (*overhears this*): I am, am I? And you think you're a hell of a lot of gentlemen, because you're politicians and Christians and other breeds of liberals. Let me tell you this—in the real prison, we chaps stuck together. We weren't milksops like you. If one of our fellows had squealed on another, like Mueller did on that swine Herder the other day, he'd have spat blood the same evening.

(*During the last few words,* FRITZ GERTE, *the new commandant has come in, followed by* CORPORAL LUEDEKE *and a few S.S. men.*)

CORPORAL LUEDEKE: Barrack Seven for inspection, sir.

EGON FREUNDLICH (*drawing himself up and addressing his squad*):
Barrack Seven, 'shun. (*He turns to* FRITZ GERTE *and salutes.*)
Heil Hitler!

FRITZ GERTE: Anything to report?

EGON FREUNDLICH: Three men ill. Five in detention cells. Two
new arrivals.

FRITZ GERTE: Anything else?

CORPORAL LUEDEKE: Johann Herder, who calls himself a Bible
scholar, was ordered twenty-five lashes on the buttocks and
neck by the former commandant, sir.

FRITZ GERTE: On what grounds?

CORPORAL LUEDEKE: Because, (*reads from his notebook*) "while
peeling potatoes, he started making propaganda for his silly
Jehovah."

FRITZ GERTE: And?

CORPORAL LUEDEKE: Until now the punishment couldn't be given,
because Herder was in hospital, sick. He's well now.

FRITZ GERTE: Herder, step forward. (JOHANN HERDER *steps forward*) What did you say? No lies, please.

CORPORAL LUEDEKE: Twenty-five extra for any lies.

JOHANN HERDER: We were peeling potatoes. Then a phrase came
into my mind which the Apostle Paul wrote: "The seed shall
be sewn in unrighteousness but shall arise in glory. It shall be
sewn in weakness but shall arise in strength."

FRITZ GERTE: That's meant to be a threat, is it?

JOHANN HERDER: A warning, Herr Commandant. The world is
full of sin, anti-Christ rules on earth. Those are the signs of
which it says in the Bible that they precede the Day of Judgment.

FRITZ GERTE: By Anti-Christ, perhaps you meant our Leader, eh?

JOHANN HERDER: I meant the spirit of evil, sir.

FRITZ GERTE: Corporal Luedeke, carry out the sentence tomorrow
morning. The whole camp is to be present; see to it.

CORPORAL LUEDEKE: Very well, Herr Commandant.

JOHANN HERDER: I'm too old for such treatment, sir. I gave my
sons to the fatherland during the war. I'm seventy years old.

FRITZ GERTE: That's something you should have thought about before. Fall in. (JOHANN HERDER *steps back to his place*) I want you men to understand that I will have no slackness in the camp. I am in charge here and my orders are to be obeyed. In this camp you will be taught to understand what National Socialism means. The National Socialist Party will train you to be worthy of the Third Reich. We must preserve iron discipline in the ranks. Greater Germany allows no failures, no excuses, no weakness. Punishment will follow every delinquency. You will learn to realize that the State is greater than the individual. . . . As I came along just now I noticed that one of you had stepped on a flower-bed and trodden down one of the flowers. That's sheer careless brutality. As a punishment there will be special exercise before the evening meal. Corporal Luedeke, you will take over the squad. (*He turns to go, then recollecting himself, he walks up to* FRIEDRICH HALL.) I hope I won't hear any complaints about you. (FRITZ GERTE *turns abruptly and walks off, followed by the S.S. men.*)

CORPORAL LUEDEKE: Barrack Seven, stand at ease! . . . Stand easy! . . . Egon Freundlich, let me see your papers. (FREUNDLICH *hands him the notebook and they confer softly.*)

ERWIN KOHN (*whispering to* AUGUST KARSCH):How long will this go on?

AUGUST KARSCH: About three hours, to hell with it.

ERWIN KOHN: I've had nothing to eat all day.

AUGUST KARSCH: Keep your heart up, kid, the first days are the worst. Only don't show them you're afraid of them. The work on the moors is the worst. Thank your stars we're not doing that this evening.

PETER HOFER (*a middle-aged worker with a pale, suffering face*): Poor Herder, twenty-five lashes. He won't stand it.

FRIEDRICH HALL: God give him courage.

CORPORAL LUEDEKE: Silence! I'll have no whispering on parade. All right, Freundlich, you can join the ranks. (EGON FREUNDLICH *places himself at the head of the front rank.*) Now, let's see what you can do. Hold your heads up. Squad . . . 'Shun! . . .

Number! (*They do so.*) Form fours! . . . Right turn! . . . At the double—Quick march! Lead round in a circle, Freundlich. (*The prisoners are now running round in a circle.*) Keep in step, you bastards. . . . One—two. . . . One—two. . . . One—two . . . Faster. . . . One—two . . . One—two . . .

(*The lights fade out but the words of command continue in the darkness, gradually the rhythm becomes slower until it reaches a heavy, slow beat like the pounding of a mighty sledge-hammer. This beat is accompanied by the sound of spades striking hard ground—A light comes up on a party of prisoners digging. They dig their spades into the ground and raise them in rhythm to the words of command.* CORPORAL LUEDEKE *stands over them.*)

CORPORAL LUEDEKE: Stand forward, you! (ERWIN KOHN *comes to him.*) Why did you raise your spade before I gave the command?

ERWIN KOHN: I thought. . . .

CORPORAL LUEDEKE: You've no right to think. We do that for you. Back to your place. Bread and water for you this evening.

(*The light fades. The words of command continue in the darkness. A light comes up on* FRITZ GERTE.)

FRITZ GERTE: The National Socialist Party will train you to be worthy of the Third Reich. We must preserve iron discipline in the ranks. The State allows no failures, no excuses, no weakness. Punishment will follow every delinquency. The State is greater than the individual. Heil Hitler!

(*The light fades on* GERTE. *The words of command continue with the sound of the spades. A light comes up on* JOHANN HERDER.)

JOHANN HERDER: The seed shall be sown in unrighteousness but shall arise in glory. It shall be sown in weakness but shall arise in strength.

(*As the light fades on* HERDER *we hear the prisoners singing a verse from "The Song of the Moor Soldiers," very softly, the song that an unknown prisoner wrote in a concentration camp and another unknown prisoner set to music.*)

PRISONERS (*singing in a low voice*):

Melody of the Moor Soldiers

> Never night enthral a dawning
> Bounded every human pain
> And at last shall come the morning
> Home, you shall be ours again.
>   And then no more passes
>   The army of the marshes
>   To the marsh.

VOICE OF CORPORAL LUEDEKE: Silence! That song is forbidden.

(*The light comes up again on the prisoners working.* FRIEDRICH HALL *leans heavily on his spade at one side. He is gasping for breath.*)

FRIEDRICH HALL: Our father, that art in heaven, hallowed be thy name. Thy kingdom come, thy will be done on earth as it is in Heaven. Give us this day our daily bread and forgive us our trespasses, as we forgive them that trespass against—— (*He falls forward on the ground*)

CORPORAL LUEDEKE: What's happened? Stand up there!

PETER HOFER: He's fainted.

CORPORAL LUEDEKE: Shut your mug! Who asked you? (*He goes over to* FRIEDRICH HALL.) And he calls himself a man.

(He turns abruptly on the prisoners, who stand around HALL*)*
Get on with your work there. . . . One—two . . . One—two
. . . One—two . . .

*(The light fades, the words of command rise to a crescendo and
then fade away. The light comes up on the day room of Barrack
Seven. Rows of lockers line the walls but room is left for the
iron-barred windows. On the floor stands a long deal table with
benches on either side. In front of this a large urn of coffee
stands on a stool from which the prisoners are helping themselves. They stand in a long line to do this and return with their
cups to sit at the table.* EGON FREUNDLICH *is handing out the coffee to each prisoner. Supper consists of slices of bread and coffee.
Some of the better-off prisoners have margarine and sausage
purchased in the canteen.)*

EGON FREUNDLICH: I saw him in the hospital. His skin was in
shreds, his lungs pumped full of water. They put his ashes in a
locked urn and sent them to the widow with a Heil Hitler.
With a Heil Hitler!

HERMANN STELTER: Whose ashes?

AUGUST KARSCH: The bible scholar Herder's.

*(*FRIEDRICH HALL *staggers)*

PETER HOFER: Aren't you well?

FRIEDRICH HALL: Thank you. I'm better now.

AUGUST KARSCH: I know. Litten had the same thing. Weak heart.
Finally he wasn't able . . .

EGON FREUNDLICH *(interrupting him)*: Shut your dirty mug, August, or I'll shut it for you.

AUGUST KARSCH *(offended)*: A man ought to be allowed to say
what's true now and then.

KARL MUELLER *(a nervous, thin-faced man)*: Try to learn to express yourself a little more elegantly, Karsch, we don't all appreciate your lavatory smut.

AUGUST KARSCH *(sitting)*: Damned pansies!

PETER HOFER: Sit down here, Hall, you look bad.

(The prisoners have now sat down)

HERMANN STETLER: Two hundred men are going to be released
on the fifteenth, so I heard.

ERWIN KOHN: Do you think I've a chance?

HERMANN STETLER: Depends on what's written on your file.

ERWIN KOHN: What could be written there, except that I was an emigrant?

PETER HOFER: Probably it says the same as the rest—"no interest attached to the release of this prisoner."

ERWIN KOHN: But why? What have I done?

PETER HOFER: Ask the gentlemen themselves that. They're the only ones who know.

AUGUST KARSCH: Probably didn't like the shape of your nose, kid, and if that's the entry go and look for a rope before they hand you one.

ERWIN KOHN (*nervously*): You're joking, aren't you?

AUGUST KARSCH (*shrugs his shoulders and turns to* STETLER): Here, you fat-bellied son of bitch, hand me some of your margarine. We're all equal here, you know.

EGON FREUNDLICH: Someone's pinched that half-loaf of bread out of my locker. Is it you, Karsch?

AUGUST KARSCH: Well, you stole it from Herder, anyway.

EGON FREUNDLICH: Damned liar! (*He rises, his fists clenched*)

AUGUST KARSCH: Not so quick with your hands, pal, I've knocked a few fellows off in my time.

PETER HOFER: Shut up, the pair of you! Have you nothing better to do than bash your own silly faces?

KARL MUELLER: What do they want to quarrel for? Don't we have to see enough violence without that?

AUGUST KARSCH: Yes, you lousy milk-squirt, that's why you spend your time sucking up to our watch-dogs. You haven't the guts of a flea.

PETER HOFER: None of us are without fear anyway.

KARL MUELLER: We should try to fit ourselves into the conditions of our existence. There's no use running against the tide. That's what I think anyway.

EGON FREUNDLICH (*sarcastically*): You know they want chaps like you in Germany. Brains in your feet, obedience in your blood and the swastika on your heart.

AUGUST KARSCH: Yes, if he had an Aryan grandfather. But he didn't. His grandmother cross-bred.

KARL MUELLER: That's a libel.

AUGUST KARSCH: Oh, yes? Then, why are you still in here?

EGON FREUNDLICH: If you possessed the brains of a mouse, you'd have told them your grandmother took an Aryan lover. (*The prisoners laugh. Some of them get up and sit on the floor against the lockers*)

ERWIN KOHN: God! If I could only get out of this.

PETER HOFER: What on earth induced you to come back here, when you were safely in Paris?

ERWIN KOHN (*shrugs his shoulders*): Every morning in Paris I went for a walk in the Bois de Boulogne. That's a park, like the Tiergarten in Berlin. One morning, in April, I saw the buds on the branch of a tree, it smelt of spring and the people were happy and laughing for no reason. I don't know why, but I felt homesick. I couldn't bear the idea of the people all talking a foreign language. I saw the birches on the Wannsee, and I smelt the sand of the Mark and the pine woods. I ran back to the Hotel, packed my bag, borrowed my railway fare and came back. Can you understand that?

PETER HOFER: No. I don't yearn for a prison.

ERWIN KOHN: Isn't it your fatherland also?

PETER HOFER: My fatherland is wherever there is freedom.

ERWIN KOHN: I didn't want to believe any longer what was written in the French newspapers. It isn't possible, I said to myself, it isn't possible. You've known these people, Mueller of the Landsbergerstrasse and Schmidt of Friedrichshain; they were kind-hearted men who lived and let live, they can't have become murderers and sadists over night. I felt I had to see Schmidt and Mueller again, they'd shake my hand. "Hallo, you old runaway," they'd say, and then we'd go to Aschinger on the Alexanderplatz and have a beer. . . .

AUGUST KARSCH (*teasingly to* ERWIN KOHN): There was one Jew here whom they boiled, salted, and pickled.

ERWIN KOHN (*becoming hysterical*): I can't stand it any longer. I

can't! I thought they'd understand. I tried to make them . . .
they laughed at me. Oh, God, let me out of here, let me out!
(*He starts sobbing.*)

PETER HOFER: Steady there!

AUGUST KARSCH: Stop that! We can't allow that kind of stuff.
(KOHN *continues sobbing*) Did you hear what I said to you?
Stop that blubbering at once or I'll lay you out.

ERWIN KOHN (*lifting his head weakly*): I'm sorry.

AUGUST KARSCH (*clumsily laying his hand on* KOHN's *shoulder*):
You'll soon settle down, kid. But don't start that stuff again.
Bad for the nerves. (*He joins a fellow prisoner on the other
side of the room.*)

ERWIN KOHN (*to* PETER HOFER): You see I want to get out so badly.
There's so many things I want to paint.

PETER HOFER: Perhaps you'll be out before long. Then you can look
up my old woman and tell her I used to be damned scared of
her scoldings and squabbling.

ERWIN KOHN: Why do you say used to be? You talk as though
you were dead already.

PETER HOFER: Well, I am as good as. But they haven't the kindness to hang me.

ERWIN KOHN: Are you a Red?

PETER HOFER: First they wanted to wheedle me to come over to
them as most of my group did, then they tried to knock the
belief in Hitler into me. But they didn't succeed.

ERWIN KOHN: What's the point of being true to something, if no
one listens to you?

PETER HOFER: I listen to myself, isn't that good enough?

ERWIN KOHN: You yourself said that most of them went over.

PETER HOFER: They even went so far as to denounce me, the poor
devils.

(THE PRISONERS *clear away their dishes and go to their bedroom,
except* FRIEDRICH HALL *and* PETER HOFER.)

FRIEDRICH HALL: Why do you call the denouncers "poor devils"?

PETER HOFER: Because they trusted themselves to do more than
they were able to carry out. The spirit was willing, but the flesh
was weak. Yes, if only we'd known what was to come. We

laughed and bragged and believed in nothing—not in freedom nor in the children's bogey of the Third Reich. We called freedom a petit bourgeois phrase, so little did we know what slavery is.

FRIEDRICH HALL: Wasn't that the fault of your leaders?

PETER HOFER: It doesn't seem as simple as that to me, Herr Pastor. It's the fault of all of us, both leaders and people. We thought that if someone was a worker, then he was everybody, the Lord God himself, if you'll excuse my saying so. But workers are also only human beings, and if a man brings his pay envelope home to mother every Saturday, that doesn't make him any the wiser. Sometimes it even makes him more stupid, because he's never learnt anything, and because he falls for every swindle and doesn't see a yard beyond his nose.

FRIEDRICH HALL: Just as Esau sold his birthright for a mess of pottage, so today man sells his freedom for his daily bread. . . . Perhaps we shouldn't accuse political systems so much as pity humanity which breaks down, because men demand justice without being just, and brotherhood without having brotherly love.

PETER HOFER: That's too Christ-like for me. Please don't be offended at my saying so.

FRIEDRICH HALL: If you had the power, would you take revenge and martyr and torture your enemies?

PETER HOFER: Kill, if need be, yes. Skin them, no.

FRIEDRICH HALL: I also knew a time when I believed in power. When the war broke out, I could have served in the Red Cross or have done my duty as army chaplain. I didn't want to. I doubted the truth of the saying that I must hold out my right cheek to him who struck the left. The fatherland was threatened. For two years I fought in the trenches. For two years I gritted my teeth. It's necessary, I said to myself again and again, when I groaned with horror. I was wounded. In the hospital, a French Catholic priest was lying beside me, a soldier like me; we talked to one another. A fortnight earlier we hated and wished to kill each other. He died. On his death bed he prayed for my forgiveness. And I, my dear friend, wept and prayed

God for forgiveness. Today I believe only in the way of understanding and of love. There's no question on earth which can't
be settled without force, however complicated and entangled
it may be.

PETER HOFER: It takes two to arrive at a solution without force,
Herr Pastor. It isn't we who invite force, it's the others. Shall I
be robbed of my right and say thank you very much? I'd rather
die.

FRIEDRICH HALL: The courage to die has become cheap, so cheap
that I often ask myself whether it isn't a flight from life.

PETER HOFER: You pour the baby out with the bath. What matters
is what a man lives for and how he dies, Herr Pastor. There's
the rub. . . . In this camp there was a man, called Erich
Muehsam, and he was a poet. His crime? That he upheld the
cause of the people, that he believed in freedom and justice
for all. The Nazis couldn't forgive him that, that's why
they maimed him till he died, and when he was dead hanged
up his body and said that he'd taken a rope and hanged
himself.

FRIEDRICH HALL: Terrible!

PETER HOFER: When once these walls fall down, so much that is
terrible will come to light that it will be like Gethsemane. The
sun will darken, and the beasts will howl. Before Muehsam
died, the Nazis played a joke on him. One day they came into
his cell, took him out and pushed him against the wall. They
released the safety catches of their revolvers and one of them
said, "Now, Muehsam, you sing us a song, the Horst Wessel
Lied; we know very well that you're a famous operatic singer."
Muehsam was silent. "What, you swine, you refuse to obey?
If you don't sing, we shoot you." Muehsam was silent. There-
upon they put a spade in his hands and told him to dig his
grave. As I said, it was only a joke. Muehsam dug, without
saying a word and without flickering an eyelash. They watched
him for a time, as you know they were just joking, then they
put him against the wall once more and cried: "This is getting
too stupid for us, either you sing, or we shoot." They raised
their guns and counted. It wasn't a joke for Muehsam. He

thought his last hour had come. And do you know what he did? He sang. But he didn't sing the Horst Wessel Lied. He sang the International.

FRIEDRICH HALL (*after a pause*): Yes, that is real courage. I thank you, Herr Hofer, I believe you have given me courage too.

PETER HOFER: You're a rebel, Herr Pastor, but you don't know it.

FRIEDRICH HALL: Perhaps you're a Christian who has gone astray, and don't know it either.

(EGON FREUNDLICH *enters*.)

EGON FREUNDLICH: Get a move on! Jump to it! Step outside! Erwin Kohn for closet cleaning! Friedrich Hall for room service.

(*The* PRISONERS *hurry out of the barracks. From outside one hears orders being given and the tread of marching columns of men.* FRIEDRICH HALL *takes a brush and sweeps the dirt together. Enter an* S. S. MAN.)

S. S. MAN: Are you Hall?

FRIEDRICH HALL: Yes.

S. S. MAN: Visitors for you. (FRIEDRICH HALL *puts the broom away*.) (*Calling outside*) Ask the ladies to come this way.

(IDA HALL *and* CHRISTINE HALL *come in.* IDA HALL *throws herself on* FRIEDRICH HALL *and embraces him*.)

IDA HALL: Friedrich!

FRIEDRICH HALL: Ida! Christine!

IDA HALL: Friedrich, dear, are you well?

FRIEDRICH HALL: Yes, Ida.

IDA HALL: The gentlemen were all so friendly to us, we didn't have to announce our visit. The General managed to get us leave. They showed us in at once. I imagined it all being much worse; why, you've even got flower beds. Everyone sends you greetings, the General's doing what he can, but unfortunately he's so indiscreet that even his old friends in the ministry are worried. Goodness, I'm forgetting all the things we've brought with us. Here's one of those sponge cakes you like so much, Julie baked it for you. And here are some clean shirts. I've brought a cold sausage for you as well, you ought to put it on ice, of course, though you won't have an ice box; put it on the window sill, then it won't spoil.

FRIEDRICH HALL: Yes, my dear. Now tell me how you are. And Christine! why aren't you in America?

CHRISTINE HALL: Werner went on, father.

FRIEDRICH HALL: And you are going to follow him, is that it?

CHRISTINE HALL: We'll all go there, when you come home, father.

FRIEDRICH HALL: Yes, and we'll take the musical clock with us. But I don't like your not leaving with Werner as we arranged.

IDA HALL: She can't marry him just yet anyhow, Friedrich.

FRIEDRICH HALL: Why? What's this? Has anything come between you?

CHRISTINE HALL: No, nothing, father—only, we won't discuss it now we've so little time.

IDA HALL: They told us at the Ministry of the Interior, that you'd soon be out, and that you're a model worker. What work do they make you do, dear?

FRIEDRICH HALL (*after a painful pause*): Ida, dear, you look so pale. Haven't you been well?

IDA HALL (*unable to maintain her assumed cheerfulness*): Oh, Friedrich.

FRIEDRICH HALL: No, Ida, don't cry. I couldn't bear that. How are all my friends?

IDA HALL: We don't see very much of them now, Friedrich.

FRIEDRICH HALL: Yes, it's only in trouble that one knows who are one's real friends.

CHRISTINE HALL: The poor people of the parish pray for your safe return, papa darling. I think they miss you most of all.

FRIEDRICH HALL: Tell them to believe in me and in the word I preached to them. I, too, shall pray for them.

IDA HALL: Friedrich, if you signed that form, saying that from now on you will always obey the Leader, I believe they would release you.

FRIEDRICH HALL: I have always rendered unto Caesar that which is Caesar's. I will go on doing so.

IDA HALL: Hasn't life taught you anything?

FRIEDRICH HALL: Yes, Ida. Here in this concentration camp it's taught me that I am on the path of righteousness.

S. S. MAN: You must say good-bye now—the visiting hour is up.

IDA HALL: Don't be headstrong, Friedrich, I entreat you. Are you so sure what is God's and what is Caesar's?

S. S. MAN: The visiting hour is up.

IDA HALL: Be sure you keep warm, Friedrich, you catch cold so easily. Do they look after you here? And take a walk in the fresh air every day. And rest your eyes. Don't stay up at night so long reading. Good-bye, Friedrich. I think of you day and night, and I pray God that you come home safe and sound.

FRIEDRICH HALL (*embracing* IDA): Be strong, Ida.

CHRISTINE HALL: Good-bye, father.

FRIEDRICH HALL: Good-bye, my dear child. I'm anxious about you.

CHRISTINE HALL: No, don't worry about me, father.

FRIEDRICH HALL: Look after your mother. (*Softly*) Guard her from that "true friend."

(IDA HALL *and* CHRISTINE HALL *go out, accompanied by* S. S. MEN. *A few seconds' pause.* FRIEDRICH HALL *stays looking at the parcels. The* S. S. MAN *has returned, without* FRIEDRICH HALL *noticing him.*)

S. S. MAN: If I can help you in any way, Pastor.

FRIEDRICH HALL (*startled*): Aren't you forbidden to speak to prisoners?

S. S. MAN: You confirmed me, Herr Pastor.

FRIEDRICH HALL: Aren't you Heinrich Degen?

S. S. MAN: Yes, Herr Pastor.

FRIEDRICH HALL: Why are you a National Socialist?

S. S. MAN: When I left school, I started looking for work. For four years I was looking for work. Wherever I went they said, We're getting rid of workers, not taking them on. A man needs something which he can stand by, some bit of hope. Years went by, the only thing I learnt was having my relief card stamped. . . . Then I heard Hitler speak, Hitler said things are done like this and now you know, and even if you die of it you can be proud because many will have to die, and Germany will go on living.

FRIEDRICH HALL: Is Germany living?

S. S. MAN: It's damned different from what I thought it was going to be. I never imagined that I'd ever have to stand guard over you. (*with suppressed wildness*) One hardly dare breathe any more. Still what can one do? I don't want to be beheaded.

FRIEDRICH HALL: God give you courage.

S. S. MAN: Me? It is you who will need the courage, Herr Pastor.

FRIEDRICH HALL: I have it, now.

S. S. MAN (*coming close to* FRIEDRICH HALL): There is a spot I know of in the barbed-wire fence where the electric current has been turned off . . .

FRIEDRICH HALL: No, my friend, I am prepared for the worst that can happen to me.

S. S. MAN: Death is not the worst, Herr Pastor. Remember Johann Herder.

FRIEDRICH HALL: Yes, I know. I know. I'm afraid of that . . . terribly afraid. . . . But I must be strong, do you understand Degen? This is something that is required of me. I must bear everything.

S. S. MAN (*moving to the window*): The commandant is coming. (*softly to* FRIEDRICH HALL) Don't forget, Herr Pastor. I can help you if you want. (*His voice suddenly becomes hard as* FRITZ GERTE *comes in*) What sort of a pig-sty do you think this is? Clean up this mess and get a move on. (*Turns and salutes* GERTE) A prisoner doing room duty, sir.

FRITZ GERTE: Thank you. You may go. (*The* S. S. MAN *goes*) I'd like to say a few words to you, unofficially.

FRIEDRICH HALL (*at attention*): At your service, Herr Commandant.

FRITZ GERTE: Please forget, for a few minutes, that I'm your superior officer. You aren't a young man any longer, Pastor Hall. This camp is hard and we can't make exceptions. I've released you from closet-cleaning and from service on the moor. That's all I can do.

FRIEDRICH HALL: Thank you.

FRITZ GERTE: But I can't go on favoring you for any length of time, you must be clear about that. I've told your wife that, she understands me. (FRIEDRICH HALL *listens attentively*) You've got twenty men and women into trouble with your snivelling letters, isn't that enough? They've all been arrested and it's your fault.

FRIEDRICH HALL: I remember having received the letters, but not having written them.

FRITZ GERTE: There's no difference. The letters which someone receives, could also have been written by him. Why must you mix yourself up in politics? Christ himself said that his kingdom was not of this world.

FRIEDRICH HALL: Do you really expect me to enter into theological controversies with you? . . . Excuse my arrogance, Herr Commandant, I am ready to answer even you.

FRITZ GERTE: Why do you make life so difficult for yourself? You could live honored and respected, if only you were reasonable.

FRIEDRICH HALL: Yes, I know. I ought to keep silent. Silence would be the greatest crime.

FRITZ GERTE: I learnt in school that the Church also rooted out its enemies with fire and sword. Was that loving your neighbor?

FRIEDRICH HALL: The heads of the Church were men like you and I. Many stumbled, many erred, many have falsified his word in their blind zeal—but Christ was always the ultimate judge and Christ did not err.

FRITZ GERTE: Is that meant to be a rebuff to our Leader? (FRIEDRICH HALL *continues his sweeping*) Well, Christ was a human being too, probably a decent one.

FRIEDRICH HALL: Even though born of Jewish parents?

FRITZ GERTE: Christ hated the Jews as only a Nordic man can hate them. He turned them out of the Temple and they denounced and crucified him.

FRIEDRICH HALL: You see, you demand from me not only that I should be silent, but that I should approve of your teachings, your heresies.

FRITZ GERTE: I don't demand anything of you. Think of your wife and your daughter and submit to the inevitable. We are stronger than you, we've conquered the people, we are victors.

FRIEDRICH HALL: We can do nothing against the truth, only for the truth.

FRITZ GERTE: Sign the form saying that you will obey Hitler, and I guarantee that you will be released.

FRIEDRICH HALL: So long as Hitler observes the law I shall obey him, freely and without signing any forms. I have no more desire to escape the arm of authority than had the Apostles of old. But nor will I keep quiet at man's behest when God commands me to speak. We must obey God rather than man.

FRITZ GERTE: Look here, Hall, don't make things so damned difficult. Remember I may one day be your son-in-law.

FRIEDRICH HALL: Is that why little Christine has not gone to America? Are you still trying to blackmail my family?

FRITZ GERTE: Without my help your wife would now be in jail for smuggling currency.

FRIEDRICH HALL: Your arm reaches far, Herr Commandant. . . . But while I have words in my mouth and truth in my heart Christine will never marry a hangman's slave.

FRITZ GERTE (*furious*): Silence!

FRIEDRICH HALL (*his excitement growing*): There will be no more silence now, Herr Commandant. You and I stand face to face, unmasked in the sight of God. The words that I will speak belong not to me but to another and they shall be spoken. I call you a hangman's slave with good reason.

FRITZ GERTE: Silence, you damned fool. If others overhear you I shall have to sentence you to be lashed.

(CORPORAL LUEDEKE's *voice from outside—"Barrack Seven back from outdoor duty."*)

FRIEDRICH HALL: I dare you to do it. The others are here. The time has come.

FRITZ GERTE (*between his teeth*): Hall, I implore you. . . .
(*The prisoners come in.*)

FRIEDRICH HALL (*loud and calm*): Fellow men, I denounce this man in the name of God and with him I denounce the Party, which bids him do such things (*He turns to* FRITZ GERTE) You have ordered the seventy-year-old Bible scholar Herder . . .

FRITZ GERTE (*hissing*): You're beyond saving!

FRIEDRICH HALL: . . . to be flogged because in his agony and despair he quoted a word from the Holy Scripture, to comfort himself and the others. You forced him to count the lashes and you forced us to look on at his martyrdom. Herder has died. An hour will come, Fritz Gerte, when you will answer for this if not before your earthly judges, then before your heavenly ones.

FRITZ GERTE: Guard!

S. S. MAN HEINRICH DEGEN: Yes, sir!

FRITZ GERTE: Put the prisoner into solitary confinement. To-morrow morning he will receive twenty-five strokes before the assembled camp.

(FRITZ GERTE *and* CORPORAL LUEDEKE *go out quickly*.)

S. S. MAN HEINRICH DEGEN (*softly to* FRIEDRICH HALL *as he leads him out*): We can do it now, Herr Pastor. It's your only chance.

FRIEDRICH HALL: God give me courage.

(*The* S. S. MAN *goes out with* FRIEDRICH HALL)

KARL MUELLER: He must have gone mad.

EGON FREUNDLICH: Well, his number's up.

AUGUST KARSCH: Damned fool to start preaching like that. Thank God an enlightened old proletarian like me doesn't get fooled by religion.

PETER HOFER: Shut up, the lot of you! If only Germany had had more like him.

ERWIN KOHN (*softly*): My mother was a servant woman too.

(*There is a short pause*)

AUGUST KARSCH (*rousing himself*): Guess you're right, pal. We're all a lot of lousy cowards really.

PETER HOFER: Well, let's have the song. . . .

EGON FREUNDLICH: Come on—the "Song of the Moor Soldiers."

KARL MUELLER: Not that, not that. It's forbidden.

SEVERAL PRISONERS: Damned coward! Shut your mouth! Why didn't you stay with your mama? With his grandmama, more likely!

EGON FREUNDLICH (*to* MUELLER): Listen, you lousy, sneaking son of a milk-sucking Portugese, if you attempt to squeal once again, I'll give you a rubbing down with my own hands that'll teach you, there are some things a gentleman doesn't do. Understand?

(KARL MUELLER *goes off into the bedroom and sits down with his back to the others. The other prisoners begin to sing. At first softly then gradually louder, with suppressed rebelliousness.*)

PRISONERS (*singing*):

> Further than the eye can follow
> Moor and marsh encompass me
> Lifeless every hagg and hollow
> Cold and crooked every tree
> > The army of the marshes
> > with pick and shovel passes
> > To the marsh.
>
> Bleak the winter sun has westered
> From the barbed and wounding wire
> To the prison camp sequestered
> We are far from our desire.
> > The army of the marshes
> > with pick and shovel passes
> > To the marsh.
>
> Never night enthral a dawning
> Bounded every human pain
> And at last shall come the morning
> Home, you shall be ours again.
> > And then no more there passes
> > The army of the marshes
> > To the marsh.*

(*During the singing of the last stanza, the prison sirens begin to whistle.*)

CALLS FROM OUTSIDE: Away from the windows! Away from the windows!

(*The rattle of a machine gun and rifle shots are heard. Great disturbance among the prisoners*)

PETER HOFER: The sirens! Someone has fled!

---

* Translated by W. H. Auden.

EGON FREUNDLICH: The parson!

HERMANN STETLER: Out and out suicide.

AUGUST KARSCH: He's dead by now.

KARL MUELLER: We'll have to pay for it.

ERWIN KOHN (*intensely*): Schema Jisroel, adenoi elohem, adenoi echod.

PETER HOFER (*who has crept to the window, turning round*): They've shot an S. S. man—it's Heinrich Degen.

CURTAIN

ACT THREE

ACT THREE

The following day.
Living room in General Paul von Grotjahn's house.
In the background, right of the audience, doors. Heavy oak furni-
ture and leather-covered chairs. Over the writing table there
hangs a big picture of King Frederic II. Over a low book shelf a
picture by Anton Werner, "Founding of the German Reich at
Versailles." On the writing table there stands a bronze lion. In
one corner, on a high pedestal, the bust of the Venus of Milo.
Room and writing desk are painfully clean and orderly. Pencils,
arranged in a row like soldiers, lie on the desk which is empty
of papers and books. At times, while the General is speaking, he
takes a pencil and puts it in line, only a soldier would under-
stand why.
TRAUGOTT PIPERMANN *stands in front of the General, who is sitting*
at his writing desk.
PAUL VON GROTJAHN: What can I do for you, Herr . . . ?
TRAUGOTT PIPERMANN: Pipermann, Excellence, Traugott Pipermann.
PAUL VON GROTJAHN: Herr Pipermann.
TRAUGOTT PIPERMANN: Although I wanted to serve the fatherland,
yet the doctors refused me on account of a chronic ulcer of the
stomach. I wanted to underline that, because there are evil
tongues wagging. The ulcer still gives me trouble.
PAUL VON GROTJAHN: Interesting, Herr. . . .
TRAUGOTT PIPERMANN: Excellence, have you really and truly forgotten who I am? Although on that memorable day my eyes
were naked and today I'm wearing blue spectacles and where
the stomach's amiss the eyes are amiss also, yet they're only
glasses for preserving my sight.

65

PAUL VON GROTJAHN: Damned if I ever saw you before in my life . . . what d'you say the name was?

TRAUGOTT PIPERMAN: Pipermann. Your excellency ordered from me, when your blessed wife was still living, a pair of shoes in brown patent leather, with rubber soles. Although I was of the opinion that brown patent leather would have a tendency to crease into little folds, yet I believe that I served your excellency conscientiously.

PAUL VON GROTJAHN: Of course, the shoemaker. (PIPERMANN *contorts with pain because the General calls him shoemaker and not master shoemaker.*) Pipermann.

TRAUGOTT PIPERMANN: And why, if I may ask, has your excellency withdrawn the honor of his custom from me?

PAUL VON GROTJAHN: My dear Pipermann, no offence meant. Fact is I wear factory-made shoes nowadays. Not so beautiful and elegant as yours, but cheaper!

TRAUGOTT PIPERMAN: Indeed, we've fallen on evil, evil times.

PAUL VON GROTJAHN (*thinking that the purpose of the visit is accomplished starts to rise*): Well, Pipermann, old chap, if some rich aunt leaves me something in her will, I'll be glad to . . .

TRAUGOTT PIPERMANN (*interrupting*): Who for example would ever have thought it of Pastor Hall?

PAUL VON GROTJAHN (*attentive*): Have you news of Pastor Hall?

TRAUGOTT PIPERMANN: Although I'm only a mediator . . . mastershoemaker, yet in my free hours I'm Churchwarden of the parish. I've seen it coming. My warning was cast on the winds, and unfortunately, unfortunately Pastor Hall was also cast on the winds. Now it's too late.

PAUL VON GROTJAHN: Speak out man. Don't sit mumbling that damned nonsense. Has something happened to Hall?

TRAUGOTT PIPERMAN: Although the Bible says, let thy word be yea or nay, whatever exceedeth that is evil, yet this rule only concerns questions of conscience, and I should be the last who would care to speak evil of Pastor Hall. He is a poor prisoner. The present authorities accuse him of serious failings, yes, even of crimes, and far be it from me to pass judgment on these accusations.

PAUL VON GROTJAHN: Have you come here to say anything or have you not?

TRAUGOTT PIPERMANN: Patience, Herr General, I crave your patience. It is often better to conceal our words these days, but men who seek the truth will not have difficulty in perceiving it. Now, although the parish prays for its parishoners and no one believes in the guilt of the pastor and the church is full as never before and the collection boxes too, Herr General, yet I believe that all this brings harm on the Pastor and suspicion and persecution on the parish. Loyalty is an honorable thing, Excellency, and you are a loyal friend of the Pastor's. I am also, Herr General, yet when no one follows us, would we not be better to resign ourselves and leave the just judgment to the wisdom of God?

PAUL VON GROTJAHN: Herr . . .

TRAUGOTT PIPERMANN: Pipermann, Excellency, Master-Shoemaker Pipermann.

PAUL VON GROTJAHN: Pipermann, I don't know what the blazes you are driving at, but, unless I am mistaken—you're a confounded lily-livered, yellow-faced mongrel. Stay at your cobbler's last, man, and don't attempt to address another word to me on the subject of loyalty, that is, if you don't want to be horse-whipped.

TRAUGOTT PIPERMANN (*getting up quickly*): Although after this unjust insult there's nothing left for me to say, yet I say this: The just have much to endure. (*He makes for the door.*)

PAUL VON GROTJAHN (*hurling his spectacle case after him*): And take your spectacle case with you.

(PIPERMANN *retrieves his case from the floor and collides with* CHRISTINE HALL *as she comes in.*)

PAUL VON GROTJAHN: Hullo, Christine. Get back safely? How was he, the old devil? Why, what's this? Crying?

CHRISTINE HALL: No. I think I got something in my eye.

PAUL VON GROTJAHN: Sit down, young lady, and don't tell fibs. What'll you take, a schnapps? Or some old Spanish cognac, quite as good as French. Sweeter but ladies like that. . . . (*Smacks his lips.*)

CHRISTINE HALL: No, thanks. It was so awful, I don't think I shall ever forget it. Poor papa.

PAUL VON GROTJAHN: Ida seemed to think he was quite well.

CHRISTINE HALL: He was trying so hard to prevent us being anxious about him.

PAUL VON GROTJAHN: Nonsense. I've known Hall since we stole apples together—a pair of ragamuffins. Believe me, he's tough. Won't let those fellows get him down easily.

CHRISTINE HALL: Mother worries so much. She makes herself sick worrying over it all.

PAUL VON GROTJAHN: Women all the same. Ida always one of the worst. I remember as well as I remember yesterday when you were all as well off as anyone, she piled up the larder with sausages and tinned stuff. Thought you might all starve one day.

CHRISTINE HALL: She's put the old musical clock in her bedroom and lets it go on playing day and night.

PAUL VON GROTJAHN: "The God who planted iron here
      Wanted no man as slave."
The highly treasonable song? Is she afraid of being denounced?

CHRISTINE HALL: On the contrary, she opens the window so that all the neighbors can hear it.

PAUL VON GROTJAHN: Strange.

(*Pause*)

CHRISTINE HALL: Have you any news of Werner?

PAUL VON GROTJAHN: A letter eight pages long. He writes that New York's a jungle. People run around as though they have to open up new paths through the bush every day. They mistake skyscrapers for heaven and the Stock Exchange for Jacob's Ladder. But they don't let anyone gag their mouths. That's the most important thing, isn't it? . . . Otherwise everything's going very well with him.

CHRISTINE HALL (*hesitant*): Did Werner ask after me?

PAUL VON GROTJAHN: Naturally he's sad that you've broken off the engagement.

CHRISTINE HALL: That evening, when they arrested papa, and

Werner said to me that papa really had been indiscreet, and that he ought to have thought about the people who wrote him those letters, it gave me a stab, it was exactly as though a stranger were talking to me.

PAUL VON GROTJAHN: You know his opinions.

CHRISTINE HALL: He didn't place himself at father's side. He spoke of an injustice crying to Heaven, as though he were speaking about an astronomical formula.

PAUL VON GROTJAHN: Always the same. When my poor wife ran away from me, silly woman, Werner was only a brat. I thought he'd forget her, that he didn't care. One day I saw him playing. The young devil had carved a man and woman out of wood. The man was me, the woman his mother. He gave them both a good scolding, then put them in the fire. Said it served them right. No heart, that boy.

CHRISTINE HALL: There are situations in life when we must take one side or the other, aren't there?

PAUL VON GROTJAHN: Don't believe in being objective myself. Werner got that outlook from his mother. She, poor soul, took an objective view of me and Major von Dirckstein, decided for him, ran away, regretted it ever since. Terrible!

CHRISTINE HALL: If anyone had told me a year ago that I would break off an engagement with a man I loved because he didn't think like me, I'd have laughed.

PAUL VON GROTJAHN: We're living in a strange age, my dear. Politics push their way in through the keyhole. Families divided against themselves. Can't see any end to it all.

CHRISTINE HALL: But isn't it terrible to think that Werner and I, who loved each other, should be separated because of this. If we'd been living in any other time, the situation would never have arisen. We'd have been married and probably lived happily, knowing no difference between us great enough to divide us. (*After a pause*) Do you think papa would be released if I married Fritz Gerte?

PAUL VON GROTJAHN: That filthy object? Impossible. Has your mother suggested this crazy notion?

CHRISTINE HALL: No. But I know she would have liked it long ago. She doesn't talk about him any more—but somehow I feel that this is what would put everything right.

PAUL VON GROTJAHN: Don't be a damned fool, Christine. Perhaps I've no right to advise you. I don't believe in getting mixed up in people's affairs; that's why I kept clear of you and Werner. But now, confound it, I'll give you my mind. You're a straightforward girl—after my own heart—what do you want to start being a martyr for? Isn't one in the family enough for you? Daughter sacrificing herself for father. Leave that stuff to film stars and heroines of penny dreadfuls.

CHRISTINE HALL: I haven't the stuff in me to be a martyr.

PAUL VON GROTJAHN: Very well, then.

CHRISTINE HALL: I'd much rather . . .

PAUL VON GROTJAHN: Out with it.

CHRISTINE HALL: . . . Be your daughter-in-law.

PAUL VON GROTJAHN: Well, to be that, you have to include my son in the bargain.

CHRISTINE HALL: He's insufferable.

PAUL VON GROTJAHN: Now we're back where we started from.

CHRISTINE HALL: Can you explain it to me, Uncle Paul, I find Werner insufferable and yet . . .

PAUL VON GROTJAHN: You love him, eh?

CHRISTINE HALL (*softly*): Father must be freed before anything else.

PAUL VON GROTJAHN: Heaven knows, I envy that boy . . . I came damnably near proposing to you myself.

CHRISTINE HALL (*laughing*): And I'd have said yes, and then it would have been too late for you to retreat. (*Knock at the door.*)

PAUL VON GROTJAHN: Excuse me. Come in! (*Enter* JULIE, *excited and upset.*)

JULIE: I wanted to speak to Fraulein Christine.

PAUL VON GROTJAHN (*rising*): I'll go into the other room.

CHRISTINE HALL: No, wait. What is it, Julie? Has something happened to Mother?

JULIE: No, not to the Frau Pastor.

CHRISTINE HALL: Father.

JULIE: The Herr Pastor . . .

PAUL VON GROTJAHN: Say what you mean.

JULIE: The Pastor's waiting down below in a taxi.

PAUL VON GROTJAHN: You're off your nut, woman.

JULIE: It's time, sir. Oh, Fraulein Christine, he's back again, he's back again.

CHRISTINE HALL: Julie, it's not time. Where is he now, downstairs? Does mother know?

PAUL VON GROTJAHN: Just wait a moment. Let's get this straight, it may be a trap. How did it happen?

JULIE: When I was out shopping, there was a man standing at the corner who tapped me on the shoulder. I cried out in a fright, because it was dark and then I recognized the Herr Pastor . . . He said he wanted to speak to Fraulein Christine, so I told him you were here. . . . I don't think he's quite right in the head.

PAUL VON GROTJAHN: That'll do. . . . I'll go down to the taxi. (JULIE *goes out, followed by* PAUL VON GROTJAHN. CHRISTINE HALL *weeps silently. The stage remains empty for some minutes. Enter* PAUL VON GROTJAHN *and* FRIEDRICH HALL. FRIEDRICH HALL *wears a shabby peasant cloak and a worn-out hat which is too small for him. He is thin and unshaven. The flickering eyes are those of a hunted man.*)

FRIEDRICH HALL: Lock and chain the door. (*One hears the clinking of a chain and a key turning in the lock.* CHRISTINE HALL *has jumped up and, without a word, put her arms around her father. Carefully she leads him to a chair, into which* FRIEDRICH HALL *lets himself fall. By now,* PAUL VON GROTJAHN *has returned. He reaches for a glass, pours wine into it and gives it to* FRIEDRICH HALL. FRIEDRICH HALL *drinks the wine in one gulp.* PAUL VON GROTJAHN *has gone out again and returns this time with a piece of cold meat and bread and butter. Wordlessly he gives it to* FRIEDRICH HALL, *who forces himself to eat a piece, then pushes the plate away.*) I can't . . . my heart!

PAUL VON GROTJAHN: I'll have the bed made, Friedrich, you must rest. There's another day tomorrow.

FRIEDRICH HALL: Where's Ida?

CHRISTINE HALL: Probably at home, papa.

FRIEDRICH HALL: Go and fetch her, Christine. (CHRISTINE HALL *goes out. One hears again the noise of the key turning in the lock and the falling chain.*) I can't stand that sound.

PAUL VON GROTJAHN (*fills Friedrich Hall's glass and takes one for himself*): Prost, Friedrich. I drink to your health . . . and to freedom! (*Empties his glass.*)

FRIEDRICH HALL: I ran away from the camp.

PAUL VON GROTJAHN: That's what I call courage!

FRIEDRICH HALL: It wasn't courage. It was fear. Miserable fear. (*Stares before him.*)

PAUL VON GROTJAHN: Every true hero is afraid. Courage begins at the point where one overcomes fear. When I went into the barrage before Verdun, something human happened to me. I was as ashamed of myself as a nun. I was so frightened that my monocle fell out onto the ground. Then . . . I set my teeth and gave my orders with the coldest possible air.

FRIEDRICH HALL: A young man lost his life on my account.

PAUL VON GROTJAHN: Now say what happened from the beginning.

FRIEDRICH HALL: They ordered me to be punished with five and twenty lashes.

PAUL VON GROTJAHN: Scum!

FRIEDRICH HALL: I brought the punishment on myself, because I was proud and wanted to show how strong I was . . . I was led out. I went across the courtyard, and I looked up at the night sky, and the stars were far away, and I froze with cold. I began to weep and I prayed, "Lord, take this cup from me," . . . The day before I'd been forced to see them flog a seventy-year-old man. He was tied onto the trestle, two Nazis beat him with ox-hide whips. He was made to count the lashes. We all stood around in the square. When he began to scream after the tenth lash, they stuck a gag in his mouth. . . . I besought the Storm trooper who walked beside me. He took me by the arm and he led me to a place in the barbed wire fence where it wasn't electrified, and he said: "Run!" I ran. Searchlights were lit up. I saw my rescuer collapse with a bullet through him.

PAUL VON GROTJAHN (*comforting him*): Perhaps you're wrong, perhaps the fellow was only wounded.

FRIEDRICH HALL: God forgive me, that would have been still worse. They would have made him die ten deaths then.

PAUL VON GROTJAHN: Didn't they follow you?

FRIEDRICH HALL: I ran as far as the next village. A peasant took me in. He fed me, he gave me his cloak and hat, and, the next day, he drove me, covered in hay, to the outskirts of the town. (*A few seconds of silence.*)

PAUL VON GROTJAHN (*standing up*): Excuse me?

FRIEDRICH HALL: Where are you going?

PAUL VON GROTJAHN: To put on my uniform, all the decorations and orders, the Iron Cross, first class, and the whole shop window of hardware. I am going to see the Minister of War.

FRIEDRICH HALL: But, Paul, what for? There's nothing can be done now.

PAUL VON GROTJAHN: We'll see. I'm going now to insist on you're being given full liberty. If they refuse—there'll be a row, that's all.

FRIEDRICH HALL: Paul, listen to me. You'll only get yourself into trouble. You can do nothing for me now. I didn't come here for that.

PAUL VON GROTJAHN: I've been sitting on the fence too long, old boy. As Christine said to me a few minutes ago, there are situations in life, when one has to take sides. I'm going into battle now, full war kit, over the top, long live Germany!

(*During the last words, the bell rings. The door opens.* CHRISTINE HALL's *voice can be heard: "Father's in there, mama—"* IDA HALL *rushes in.*)

IDA HALL: Jesus Christ be praised!

PAUL VON GROTJAHN (*going out*): Good-bye, my dear friends.

FRIEDRICH HALL: Ida, my dear old Ida . . .

IDA HALL: Don't speak, dear heart, I know everything.

FRIEDRICH HALL: Ida, I must speak.

IDA HALL: But I know all.

FRIEDRICH HALL: I'm a fugitive, Ida, a man who's broken down, and who needs you, needs your protection, your warmth, your kind, foolish heart.

IDA HALL: We'll run away together. Somewhere we'll find a country that will take us in, and people who'll let us live and die in peace. I'm strong, I can cook and sew, I'll surely find work. You've supported me for nineteen years, now let me take care of you, little father.

FRIEDRICH HALL (*smiling tenderly*): That's what you called me on our honeymoon.

IDA HALL: I feel so gay and happy. I think it had to happen as it happened. Every sorrow has a purpose.

FRIEDRICH HALL: If we're strong enough. (CHRISTINE HALL *runs in.*)

CHRISTINE HALL: Mother, quick, Fritz Gerte is outside. He wants you.

FRIEDRICH HALL (*jumps up*): We were at least allowed to dream.

IDA HALL: Does he know?

CHRISTINE HALL: No. He heard you were here. He has been to our house.

IDA HALL (*pointing to a door on the right*): Go in there! I'll get rid of him all right. (*She pushes him through the door right.*) Ask him to come in. (CHRISTINE HALL *goes out.* IDA HALL *sits down in the chair in which* FRIEDRICH HALL *has just sat. She sits calm, upright, collected, quite a different person.* FRITZ GERTE *comes in.*)

FRITZ GERTE: So you're here. I've been looking for you like a needle in a hay stack.

IDA HALL: Won't you sit down?

FRITZ GERTE: Certainly. Thank you. Where is the General?

IDA HALL: I'd like to know that myself.

FRITZ GERTE: Are you waiting for him?

IDA HALL: Were you looking for me to ask me that question?

FRITZ GERTE: Of course not. . . . Are you well? How are you getting on?

IDA HALL: Excellently.

FRITZ GERTE: Have you heard from your husband?

IDA HALL: I visited him only yesterday.

FRITZ GERTE: Of course . . . Won't you really tell me why you're waiting for the General?

IDA HALL: If you must know it, I was going to ask him to draw up a complaint for me. I have a complaint against you.

FRITZ GERTE: Against me?

IDA HALL: Against you. Because you only allowed me a quarter of an hour in which to speak to my husband.

FRITZ GERTE: Absurd.

IDA HALL: To me, it doesn't seem at all absurd. I am going to put it through that next time I see him for an hour, perhaps even for two hours. And without surveillance.

FRITZ GERTE: You'll have to wait a long time to fix that.

IDA HALL: The General knows the Leader's Adjutant.

FRITZ GERTE: It really seems as if you know nothing.

IDA HALL: What ought I to know them?

FRITZ GERTE: Your husband's hooked it.

IDA HALL: I don't understand. . . .

FRITZ GERTE: That's his gratitude.

IDA HALL: Fled, you say? Fled abroad?

FRITZ GERTE: Possible, but not likely.

IDA HALL: Please, may I tell the news to Christine?

FRITZ GERTE: No. I've got to speak to you, Ida. I was always a good friend to you. I saved you from being sent to prison.

IDA HALL (*pointedly*): Christine's broken her engagement with Werner von Grotjahn.

FRITZ GERTE: Christine can go to the devil! Your husband's flight may cost me my life. They've already threatened me with an investigation. They'll find out that I favored him, they'll discover that I took your part. Don't you understand then, Ida, your head is in danger too.

IDA HALL: Mine? Why?

FRITZ GERTE: Because they'll find out about the smuggled money. Because they'll find out that I've been helping you. Ida, for God's sake, don't you see I'm ruined, they'll push me out of the Party.

IDA HALL: Then you'll have to take up your civil profession again.

FRITZ GERTE: I a shopkeeper? Stand behind a counter from morning till evening and sell suits off the rod? I'd sooner put a bullet through my head.

IDA HALL: Well, this time you're certain of being taken by an Aryan firm.

FRITZ GERTE: You must help me . . . and help yourself.

IDA HALL: Is it in my power?

FRITZ GERTE: Of course, it's in your power . . . I imagine that your husband's in hiding. By some means or other he'll try to get in touch with you.

IDA HALL: And then?

FRITZ GERTE: How slow you are in the uptake! As soon as you have his address, you must inform me.

IDA HALL: I must betray my husband?

FRITZ GERTE: I promise you that nothing will happen to your husband. I'll even pledge myself to get him released.

IDA HALL: You swear that to me?

FRITZ GERTE: On my word of honor.

IDA HALL: Will you give it to me in writing as well?

FRITZ GERTE (*hesitates a moment, then*): Of course. (*At this moment the door right opens and in comes* FRIEDRICH HALL. FRITZ GERTE *quickly draws out his revolver.*)

(*Speaking together*)

FRITZ GERTE: Hands up!

IDA HALL (*screaming*): Friedrich, why did you have to do this? This is the end for all of us.

FRIEDRICH HALL: No, Ida, this is perhaps the beginning, the beginning that I was afraid to face yesterday. (*turning to* FRITZ GERTE) I heard your ardent pleading just now. So powerful and yet so cowardly.

FRITZ GERTE: Cowardly? You too, Herr Pastor.

FRIEDRICH HALL: Yes, I too. I tried to shirk the trial that was laid on me . . . But now I'm coming with you. The prison cell will not drown my voice. The trestle on which you bind me will be a pulpit, and the parish so mighty that no church in the world will be able to contain it. (*The door is thrown open.* PAUL VON GROTJAHN *comes in, dressed in general's full uniform, with orders and decorations.* CHRISTINE HALL *follows him.*)

PAUL VON GROTJAHN (*calling out from the door*): Not one of the whole damned lot has any moral courage! (*Taking in the situation*) What the hell's going on?

FRITZ GERTE: Pastor Hall is my prisoner.

PAUL VON GROTJAHN: He's nothing of the sort. Pastor Hall is under my protection, I'll answer for him.

CHRISTINE HALL: Oh, papa, darling, why did you come back to this room?

FRIEDRICH HALL: Please, everyone allow me to go with this man, it's all going to be right now.

IDA HALL (*standing between* GERTE *and* FRIEDRICH HALL): I won't . . . I won't. If you dare touch him, I'll ruin you Fritz. I'll shout out what you are in the streets. I'll tell the whole story. How you bargained with me to possess Christine, how you sheltered us for your own greed and lust. I have no shame left now.

FRITZ GERTE: If it's force you want. . . . (*He pushes Ida aside at the same moment* PAUL VON GROTJAHN *seizes* GERTE'S *revolver from his other hand.*)

PAUL VON GROTJAHN: An old trick . . . Learnt it from a Frenchman . . . quite simple.

FRITZ GERTE (*moving towards the General*): How dare you . . .

PAUL VON GROTJAHN: Not so spry there. (*He levels the revolver at* GERTE): I'm master in this house and I never did like having worms like you around.

FRITZ GERTE: You'll pay for this . . .

PAUL VON GROTJAHN: Get out!

FRITZ GERTE (*shouting*): You're all under arrest.

PAUL VON GROTJAHN (*slapping* GERTE *in the face*): About turn! Quick march!

FRITZ GERTE (*stands for a moment astonished*): Even you won't get away with this, General. I'll go but not for long enough to let one of you escape. (*He turns and goes out.*)

PAUL VON GROTJAHN: Damned cheek!

IDA HALL: We must hurry. What shall we do?

PAUL VON GROTJAHN: Not much time. He'll be back. With a hundred armed thugs even that fellow might be dangerous. Come,

Friedrich. (*They turn and look at* PASTOR HALL *who stands motionless.*)

FRIEDRICH HALL: Today is Sunday.

PAUL VON GROTJAHN: We better try the backstairs.

CHRISTINE HALL: You'll have to come too, Uncle Paul.

PAUL VON GROTJAHN: They won't touch me. (*The clock strikes seven-thirty.*)

FRIEDRICH HALL (*as if in a trance*): The evening service is just going to begin.

IDA HALL: Friedrich, darling, what do you mean?

FRIEDRICH HALL (*to* VON GROTJAHN): Do you think we could get as far as the church?

IDA HALL (*understanding*): Friedrich!

FRIEDRICH HALL: My place is in the pulpit.

PAUL VON GROTJAHN: Not wise, old fellow.

FRIEDRICH HALL: Were you wise to throw Gerte out?

PAUL VON GROTJAHN: Had to do something about it.

FRIEDRICH HALL: Yes, that's it. Even you, Paul, who've remained silent for so long. You had to do something about it. Others will do the same.

CHRISTINE HALL: Papa, darling, listen to me. I've always stood by you. Even in the concentration camp, when I knew how mother was suffering because of you, I didn't beg you to give in and sign. I knew in my heart that you had to go your own way. but now what you want to do is insane.

FRIEDRICH HALL: What then? Am I to escape by the backstairs, like a common criminal?

CHRISTINE HALL: Because you have the right to live. Because we need you too.

FRIEDRICH HALL: I can't sacrifice the truth any longer, not even for you and Ida.

IDA HALL: But they won't let you preach.

PAUL VON GROTJAHN: It's open rebellion! You can't defeat them. They are in power now. Why should they give in?

FRIEDRICH HALL: Did Christ give in?

IDA HALL: But Gerte will break into the church. He'll arrest you in the pulpit.

FRIEDRICH HALL: Then three thousand people will see that their rulers are afraid of the truth.

PAUL VON GROTJAHN: Rubbish. Three thousand people will creep like Traugott Pipermann. Anyhow what is truth?

FRIEDRICH HALL: With that question Pontius Pilate tempted a Greater One.

IDA HALL: Friedrich, they'll kill you.

FRIEDRICH HALL (*very softly*): I will live. It will be like a fire that no might can put out, the meek will tell the meek and they'll become brave again. One man will tell another that the anti-Christ rules, the destroyer, the enemy of mankind—and they will find strength and follow my example.

(*For a moment there is silence. Then* IDA HALL *goes to* FRIEDRICH HALL *and embraces him.*)

CHRISTINE HALL: Let us go, father.

PAUL VON GROTJAHN: I've been proud of this uniform all my life, so was my father and his father before him. Better find someone to serve now . . . no use if you don't believe in what you're fighting for . . . (*lightly*) If you don't mind, old fellow, I'll stand beside the pulpit. Never did care for sermons much but still . . .

FRIEDRICH HALL: Thank you, Paul.

(*A short pause*)

IDA HALL: It's time. Come.

(*They leave the room. From outside comes the tolling of the church bell, which continues until the end. After a moment* JULIE *comes in, she looks around, troubled. Then from the distance comes the tramp of marching men. It grows nearer.* JULIE *kneels down and prays.*)

CURTAIN

BLIND MAN'S BUFF

by
ERNST TOLLER
and
DENIS JOHNSTON

CHARACTERS

DR. FRANK CHAVASSE
LAURA (his child)
MARY QUIRKE (his servant)
DR. ANICE HOLLINGSHEAD
DOMINICK MAPOTHER
SERGEANT CAREY
MR. JUSTICE DROOLEY
HENRY HARRICAN (Senior Counsel)
THEOBALD THIN (Barrister-at-Law)
LIAM POER (State Solicitor)
JOHN ROCHE (Solicitor)
SEAMUS UA CAOILTE (Assistant State Pathologist)
COURT REGISTRAR
CRIER
A JURYMAN
ATTORNIES, ETC.

This play was first performed in the Abbey Theatre, Dublin, on Boxing Day, 1936, with the following cast:

Dr. Frank Chavasse	ARTHUR SHIELDS
Laura	PATSY FITZPATRICK
Mary Quirke	MAY CRAIG
Dominick Mapother	F. J. McCORMICK
Dr. Anice Hollingshead	EILEEN CROWE
Sergeant Carey	P. J. CAROLAN
John Roche	ERIC GORMAN
Theobald Thin	MICHAEL J. DOLAN
Liam Poer	FRED JOHNSON
Henry Harrican	AUSTIN MELDON
Mr. Justice Drooley	TOM PUREFOY
Registrar	FRANK CARNEY
Seamus Ua Caoilte	DENIS O'DEA
Juryman	BRIAN CAREY
Attornies, etc.	Messrs. BARROR, CONSIDINE, HICKEY and FINN

The play was produced by HUGH HUNT with settings designed by TANYA MOISEIWITSCH

ACT ONE

ACT TWO

ACT THREE

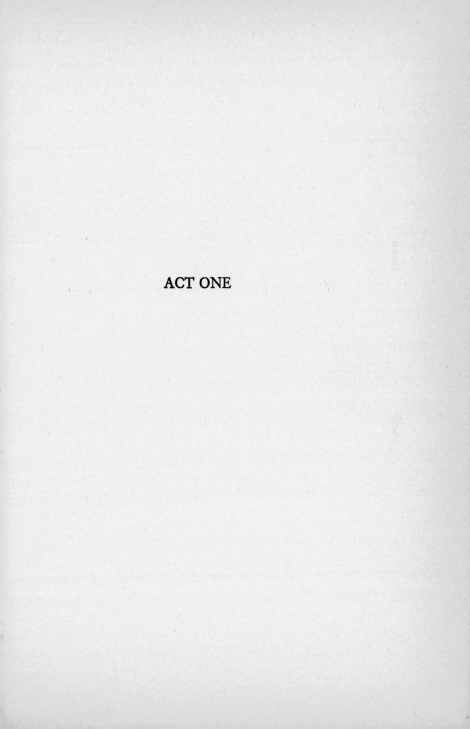

ACT ONE

ACT ONE

SCENE I

The hall of Dr. Chavasse's house in a small Irish country town. To the centre is the hall door. There are two interior doors on each side of the room—those on one side leading to the sitting-room and to the consulting room respectively and those on the other side leading to the waiting-room and to the kitchen quarters.

(MARY QUIRKE *is listening at the door of the consulting room. Presently* LAURA *enters by the hall door playing with a ball*)

LAURA: I can throw it higher than you, Mary.

MARY: Hush!

LAURA: I can throw it higher than anybody in the world, except Daddy. Daddy can throw it the highest of all.

MARY: Hush, Laura, with your poor Mother lying sick in there. What way is that to behave? Have you been in to see her?

LAURA: No.

MARY: Why not? Didn't I tell you to go in and see her?

LAURA: Don't want to.

MARY: Why you unnatural child, you! Go along with you at once and speak to your poor Mother. Maybe she'll be dead the next time!

LAURA: I'd like to wait for my Daddy. I'm afraid of people when they're sick.

MARY: Go along with you when you're told. Afraid of sick people indeed! You'll never go to Heaven—a bad child that talks like that. (*The hall door bell rings. She pushes the reluctant* LAURA *off into the sitting-room and returns to the hall door which she opens.* MAPOTHER *enters*)

MARY: Hush! What do you want, Dominick Mapother?

MAPOTHER: Good morning, my dear ma'am. Dominick salutes

you cordially. (*He speaks in a high sing-song, with his eyes fixed upon a corner of the ceiling*)

MARY: It's no good your trying to see the Doctor now. There's trouble enough here as it is.

MAPOTHER: Ah, my good woman, sorrow and misfortune is our lot here below. But believe me, if it was only for my unworthy self I'd not be intruding upon you with my importunities.

MARY: I suppose it's your poor wife. Have you been knocking her around again?

MAPOTHER: As God is my witness, ma'am dear, I've never raised a hand to her since the fatal spring of twenty-eight, when my patience last gave out under stress of domestic and particular brawls too stormy to be endured by mortal man. Ah, the whirlwinds of matrimony!

MARY: Well we've no time now for you and your whirlwinds, Dominick Mapother, what with the Mistress stretched near her death in the sitting-room.

MAPOTHER: Near her death, do you tell me ma'am? Oh, that grieves me deeply—very deeply indeed. I'll be off without demur so I will. But I wonder now if the Doctor would be easy in his mind if I were to go without the bottle of medicine he promised for my distressed establishment?

MARY: I don't know anything about it. He's busy now telephoning to that Dr. Hollingshead.

MAPOTHER: To the She-Doctor! A fine strap of a girleen I always say. Ah, but sure doctoring is an unnatural employment for one of the gentler sex.

MARY: Strap is right—with her lipstick and her college airs. No good will come of it if he's trying to bring that one over to this house.

MAPOTHER: Silence, my good woman. Let the voice of controversy and scandal be stilled in the presence of the sick and suffering. Your insinuendo has no locus standi with a Mapother.

MARY: Ah, go along with you. Or look, you can stay in the waiting-room, and maybe he'll give you a bottle for your wife when he's finished. I've no time for gostering with you.

MAPOTHER: Did you say 'wife'? Ah, God be merciful, it's not my better half that is afflicted. She is as hale and as free in the tongue as the day I took her—that moment of memorable misfortune. No ma'am, it's the cow. She's in trouble again.

MARY: Why, you rascally old gasbag, is it a cow-doctor you're looking for? I declare to God, I believe you're sorry that it isn't your wife that's ailing!

MAPOTHER: Well ma'am, will a cow answer back? Would a cow eject me out of bed of a morning with the blow of a foot into a cold and unsavoury world? Ah, ma'am, if you could see her, standing in the byre, the beads of pain upon her brow, and her sad brown eyes bursting out with the stress of her internal torments, you would never speak slightingly of one of the noblest of God's creatures—the lowly cow.

MARY (*pushing him off*): Well, maybe he'll see you and maybe he'll not. It's no concern of mine. I've got to go about my business. (*She bustles him into the waiting-room and goes off herself towards the kitchen. Presently* CHAVASSE *enters from the consulting-room. He is very agitated. He looks through the glass of the hall door and then goes to the door of the sitting-room*)

CHAVASSE: Laura! What are you doing in there! Come out at once.

(LAURA *emerges sobbing*)

CHAVASSE: What were you doing in there? What's the matter?

LAURA: I'm frightened. Mummy stared at me so queerly and made a noise. Then she tried to get off the couch at me and then she— she—

CHAVASSE: Stop crying, Laura. It was very naughty of you to go in when Mummy's not well. Don't you know that?

LAURA: Mary made me.

CHAVASSE: Mary made you?

LAURA: She said I'd die and go to hell if I didn't go in and see Mummy.

CHAVASSE: That was very wrong of Mary. There, there, dear. It's all right. I'll speak to her. There's nothing more to cry about.

LAURA: I'll have dreams, do you think?

CHAVASSE: Not a dream, dear. Hello, here's a nice ball.

LAURA: That's my ball. I can throw it higher than almost anybody.

CHAVASSE: Then out you go into the garden with it.

LAURA: Will you look out and watch me throw it, Daddy?

CHAVASSE: Yes, dear, when I've time. And don't go into the sitting-room again.

LAURA: And I can jump over the wall at the end of the garden. Can you do that, Daddy?

CHAVASSE: No, I'm sure I couldn't. Now run along, dear. That's a good girl. (*She goes out by the hall door.* CHAVASSE *hesitates at the kitchen passage tentatively, but turns and goes back into the sitting-room. Presently there is a knock at the hall door and he re-emerges and opens it.* ANICE HOLLINGSHEAD *enters*)

CHAVASSE: Anice! Oh, thank God you've come!

ANICE: Frank—you shouldn't have sent for me.

CHAVASSE: I had to, Anice. She's sinking. I can't think what to do.

ANICE: What's the matter?

CHAVASSE: I can't imagine. It looks like poison.

ANICE: Poison!—But surely—this is terrible! How can I possibly attend her? Is she conscious?

CHAVASSE: She was some time ago. But not now. She's been having recurrent spasms of coma all morning, ever since I found her. Anice, I'm distracted!

ANICE: Oh, but to telephone like that! Was that necessary?

CHAVASSE: I know. I lost my head. But what else could I do when you wouldn't answer my note?

ANICE: I never got any note.

CHAVASSE: But I sent one over to you by Mary Quirke. Didn't she give it to you?

ANICE: No. She never came.

CHAVASSE: Never came! I don't understand! She said you had no reply. What does she mean by it?

ANICE: Never mind about Mary, Frank. Tell me about Elizabeth.

CHAVASSE: Elizabeth. I found her lying there after breakfast. I tried to give her an emetic but she spat it out and then collapsed.

ANICE: Spat it out!

CHAVASSE: Then I gave her an injection and sent Mary over for you. You were the only help I could think of. It was wrong of me, I know, but what else could I do?

ANICE: Frank, could it be suicide?

CHAVASSE: Oh God, Anice, don't say that! Anice, what'll I do? You'll have to help me.

ANICE: Oh God, this isn't all going to start again, is it?

CHAVASSE: Yes, she's trying to kill herself! I knew it from her eyes —the way she looked at me when I came in.

ANICE: All right. Let me see her at once. Maybe there's something I can do.

CHAVASSE: God bless you, Anice. I knew you wouldn't let me down. I knew—

ANICE: Of course not. Is she in here? (*She goes into the sitting-room. He is about to follow her when* MARY QUIRKE *enters*)

CHAVASSE: Mary, please keep away from here when I tell you. And by the way, why did you say that Dr. Hollingshead had no answer to my letter?

MARY: Nor had she.

CHAVASSE: That's not what she tells me. She says you never delivered it.

MARY: I can't help what that one says.

CHAVASSE: Don't lie to me, Mary. And another thing, don't send Laura in to see the Mistress when you know that my instructions are that she is to be left alone.

MARY: And why wouldn't she go in and see her Mother? It's maybe the last time.

CHAVASSE: Mary, I am the best judge of what is right or proper for that child.

MARY: I wonder. That's not what the Mistress thinks.

CHAVASSE: I don't like your manner, Mary.

MARY: There's lots I don't like.

CHAVASSE: What exactly do you mean by that?

MARY: I mean what I say. Why don't you go in and attend to the Mistress yourself?

CHAVASSE: How dare you dictate to me, Mary. If you don't go back to your kitchen at once and stay there, I shall give you a month's notice.

MARY: Oh, you needn't bother to give me notice. I'll go when I choose.

CHAVASSE: You'll go when I send you, Mary Quirke. You'll go now, if I have another word out of you.

MARY: Ah, go in to your wife and leave me alone. She's the one that needs your attention, and not that strap from the Dispensary.

CHAVASSE: Get out of this at once, you impudent slut!

MARY: I don't go till I know what's wrong with the Mistress.

CHAVASSE: It's none of your business what's wrong with her.

MARY: I'm going to stay here till I find out. Lay a finger on me and I'll have the law on you.

CHAVASSE: Mary—I'll—if you don't get out of here at once—I'll—I'll fetch the police and have you put out.

MARY: I'm not afraid of the police. Why should I mind the police?

CHAVASSE: Why should you—All right, I'll show you why. You want some law do you? Well, you'll get it. (*He strides off to the telephone*)

MARY: What do you mean?

CHAVASSE (*off*): I mean that I know some things that may interest the police in you.

MARY: What things?

CHAVASSE (*off*): Ever since the Mistress has been ill, you have been taking money from me to pay the tradespeople, and I found out only yesterday that hardly one of them has been paid. Hello! Hello!

MARY: It's a lie!

CHAVASSE: You thought I'd be too busy to find out—but I have found out. So now my good woman we'll see who gets the best law.

ANICE (*off*): Please be quiet out there. Don't you know—

MARY: It's a dirty lie. I'll have the law on you for slander and defamation of my good character.

CHAVASSE (*off*): Hello! Get me the Civic Guards, please.

MARY: What call have you for to be naming me a thief—me that has worked my fingers to the bone for the poor Mistress these past five years—me that has kept the house going in winter or summer with never a thought for myself, serving you hot meals

and cold at all hours of the day and night. If they say I didn't
pay them, it's a lie—a lie!

CHAVASSE (*off*): Is that the Guards? This is Dr. Chavasse speaking. Yes. Would you kindly send down an officer at once. I wish
to make a charge of rather a serious nature. Yes, as soon as you
can, before the person can get away. Thank you, Sergeant.

ANICE (*from the next room*): Frank! Frank! Come quickly!

CHAVASSE: Coming! (*He hurries in and enters the sitting-room*)

MARY: I tell you it's the boys that's cheating and not me, and if
anyone says it's me I'll prove them a liar so I will. All right. I'm
leaving you, never fear. I'll not stay in this house to be accused
of robbery and knavery. I'm leaving you all right. I'm packing
my bag this minute and I'm off out of this. (*She goes off left as*
MAPOTHER *peers out of the waiting room*)

MAPOTHER: Oh, my dear sir, do I hear voices raised in anger? (*He
crosses right, and listens*)

CHAVASSE (*off*): Stethoscope. Quickly! Good God! Did you bring
any camphor?

ANICE (*off*): In my bag—a syringe.

CHAVASSE (*off*): Hand me that wadding. Have you a two inch
needle? It's now or never.

ANICE (*off*): Adrenalin! Her arm is moving.

CHAVASSE (*off*): On the table. Keep this quiet, for God's sake!

ANICE (*off*): I'll hold it. There. When did you give it her?

CHAVASSE (*off*): I tried a needle in the heart about an hour ago.

ANICE (*off*): Loosen her clothes. Uncover the breast again.

CHAVASSE (*off*): Did you see her blink?

ANICE (*off*): You can leave it. There's nothing more to be done.
She's dead. (*There is a pause*)

CHAVASSE (*off*): Dead! (*There is quite a long pause in complete
silence. Then* CHAVASSE *suddenly emerges and bumps into*
MAPOTHER. LAURA *enters by the hall door*)

CHAVASSE: What the devil—!

LAURA: Did you watch me running, Daddy?

MAPOTHER: Oh, my dear sir, far be it from Dominick to intrude.

CHAVASSE: What are you doing here?

MAPOTHER: Just a small matter, my dear sir. I scarcely like to mention it.

LAURA (*swinging on* CHAVASSE): I can climb up you, Daddy.

MAPOTHER: A little matter of a bottle I was to call for. An elixir for my unfortunate cow.

CHAVASSE: Oh, damn your cow! Oh, yes, I remember. Don't do that, Laura. Yes, I left it out for you over there. Please take it and go.

MAPOTHER: With alacrity, my dear sir. But alas, no bottle here.

LAURA: Now play lifts, Daddy. Ring the bell for the lift.

CHAVASSE: Oh, leave me alone, Laura. And do go away, Mapother.

MAPOTHER: It has been removed. How mortifying! No bottle for poor Dominick.

LAURA (*bursting into tears*): Yes, I took a bottle—don't be cross, Daddy. I wanted a bottle for my Teddy. I'm sorry, Daddy. It's in my dolly's pram.

CHAVASSE: That's all right—oh, do stop crying! Take Mr. Mapother and give it back to him. And don't come back in here till I send for you.

LAURA: Yes, Daddy.

MAPOTHER (*as he hurriedly leaves with* LAURA): Thank you, my dear sir. Your humble servant. Most obliged.

(*Meanwhile* ANICE *has appeared in the door right*)

ANICE: There's nothing more to be done.

CHAVASSE: Oh, my God! My God! What is it?

ANICE: Can't be sure without a post-mortem. But from the symptoms I would diagnose Sinacide.

CHAVASSE: Oh, God, what a thing for her to have done!

ANICE: Was it quite unexpected?

CHAVASSE: Oh, she has threatened it several times. But I thought it was just hysteria—I never dreamt it would come to anything.

ANICE: Then she wasn't improving?

CHAVASSE: She was getting worse every month—working herself into a complete breakdown.

ANICE: Not because of us?

CHAVASSE: Ever since she found out.

ANICE: But she must have known that it was all over—that we've never even spoken for nearly two years.

CHAVASSE: That didn't seem to make any difference. It was an obsession with her. She had made up her mind that I was going to leave her and she fretted herself sick with hatred.

ANICE: Poor Elizabeth. She should have known you better. But why didn't you tell me? I could have gone away.

CHAVASSE: Thrown up your job? No, Anice. I've been responsible for enough without that as well. I offered to sell out and take her away, but she wouldn't agree. No divorce—no separation—no going away. It was you who must go.

ANICE: I understand. It was a matter of pride with her. It was I who had done the wrong.

CHAVASSE: I wouldn't let her ruin you, Anice! I saw to that anyhow.

ANICE (*with a wry smile*): That was nice of you, Frank.

CHAVASSE: And so she got worse and worse in spite of all I could do. Oh, Anice, it has been hell—all these months!

ANICE: Poor Frank! You should have told me.

CHAVASSE: Not being able to speak to you—nobody to talk to—

ANICE: I know, dear. We tried to do something that can't be done. We tried to live on, as though the past had never existed. We thought that we could just ignore it.

CHAVASSE: I was a fool. I should have made you come away with me.

ANICE: No, Frank. We could never have carried it off. I haven't any illusions that we would ever have been happier.

CHAVASSE: But now we can be together at last—free from her hate—free from—But, oh my God, can we? There'll be an inquest now. It will all come out! People will want to know . . .

ANICE: Steady, Frank!

CHAVASSE: No, it will be worse than ever, now. What shall we do? It was her last act of venom. Oh, I should never have gone for you!

ANICE: Be calm, dear.

CHAVASSE: I saw it in her eyes when I came in and found her lying there. She didn't answer when I spoke to her. But she looked at me and I could see that she knew that she had won.

ANICE: I can't blame her for hating me. But if only she had realized how well she was revenged already it might have been easier for her.

CHAVASSE: It was her trump card, and how well she knew how to play it! She would never have left me any other way. She must live on to make our lives a hell, and then go out like this. Curse her! Curse her! Curse her!

ANICE: For God's sake stop, Frank. It's horrible!

CHAVASSE: But I'll beat her yet. If only we can hush this up we'll beat her yet. Yes, that's the thing to do.

ANICE: What do you mean?

CHAVASSE: Hasn't she been ailing for months? Everybody knows it. But they don't know what's been the matter with her. Why need they know now?

ANICE: But they're bound to know. There'll be a post-mortem.

CHAVASSE: Why should there? Why need it be poison? Supposing it were something else . . . say gastro-enteritis . . . why need there be a post-mortem?

ANICE: But it isn't, and there'll have to be a death certificate.

CHAVASSE: Which you can give as a matter of course.

ANICE: Frank, I couldn't do that. It would be utter madness.

CHAVASSE: Anything else would be madness. My God, why should anybody question it? You're a qualified independent Dispensary Doctor. I've called you in and you've examined her. Anice, you must certify her.

ANICE: It's impossible. Goodness knows what would happen if we tried such a thing.

CHAVASSE: This is what will happen. We'll beat her after all. We'll prevent her ruining our lives with a scandal that would drive us both out of practice. Why, in six months time she'll be forgotten and we can get married and start a new life together at last.

ANICE: Oh, Frank, please don't ask me.

CHAVASSE: We belong to each other. We need each other.

ANICE: I wonder, Frank. Oh, I wonder.

CHAVASSE: But surely you don't doubt it, dear? After all that we have been through.

ANICE: That's just it. We've been through nothing. Oh, it isn't as though I hadn't thought it over and over during these past months. Sometimes I've thought that you did the right thing . . . the only thing. And then again I've found myself wondering what reality there could have been in a love that ended so . . . so sensibly?

CHAVASSE: Do you blame me for that?

ANICE: I don't want to be selfish or unjust, Frank. But sometimes I can't help asking myself what you would have done if it hadn't turned out the way it did.

CHAVASSE: You mean, if the child had been born?

ANICE: Weren't you just a little glad that it wasn't necessary to find a way out?

CHAVASSE: Anice, you're cruel! Don't you believe in me?

ANICE: I think so, Frank. I want to, oh so much. But perhaps it was just as well that we didn't have to put our love to the test. Oh Frank, why can't we let it be?

CHAVASSE: Oh God, is this a time to speak to me like that? Have I lost you too? I know what you've suffered. But do you think that I haven't suffered as well? I can't bear it. If you're going to let me down now, I don't know what I'll do. (*He commences to sob*)

ANICE: There, there. I know, darling. I understand.

CHAVASSE: It's been a living torment knowing you were there and remembering what we had lost. All that I'd left was your old letters. I used to sit alone at night going over them and wondering whether we'd done right . . . whether there was any other way out. What else could I have done?

ANICE (*comforting him*): I know. Of course you did what you thought was best for both of us. What more could one ask?

CHAVASSE: I can't face this without you.

ANICE: There. We'll face it together. (*She kisses him and he holds her to him. Somebody glances through the glass at the side of the hall door and then rings the bell. They spring apart*)

CHAVASSE: There's someone at the door.

ANICE: Open it.

CHAVASSE (*glancing out*): It's the police. I sent for them.

ANICE: It'll be all right, dear. Keep your head. (*She goes back into the adjoining room, as* CHAVASSE *admits* SERGEANT CAREY)

CAREY: Good afternoon, Doctor.

CHAVASSE: Oh, hello, Sergeant.

CAREY: You sent for me, sir?

CHAVASSE: Why yes, of course.

CAREY: Some trouble in the house?

CHAVASSE: Oh, just some petty pilfering by a servant. I wanted to teach her a lesson, but I don't think I shall make any formal charge.

CAREY: I understand, sir. You'd just like me to say a few words to her.

CHAVASSE: Quite so. A scare will do her good. But another time, I think, Sergeant. I'm rather upset at the moment. You see, Mrs. Chavasse has just died.

CAREY: You don't tell me that, sir! 'Tis sorry I am indeed to hear it.

CHAVASSE: Yes. She collapsed less than an hour ago.

CAREY: Very sudden. But I've heard tell she's been ailing for some time, sir. So maybe it wasn't unexpected?

CHAVASSE: Er . . . no indeed, Sergeant.

CAREY: Very sad. What was the trouble, sir?

CHAVASSE: The stomach. Gastro-enteritis, I'm afraid, followed by cardiac collapse. I called in Dr. Hollingshead and she has just completed her examination. She's in there now.

CAREY: Well, I'm sure, Doctor, you have the sympathy of one and all in your loss. (ANICE *enters*) Good afternoon, Doctor. I was just telling the Doctor here that the whole town will be with him over this.

ANICE: Yes, Sergeant. Of course.

CHAVASSE: So I think perhaps, another time, Sergeant.

CAREY: Indeed, I understand well, sir. (MARY QUIRKE *enters with her suit case*)

MARY: It's a lie, I'm telling you. It's a dirty lie! I never touched a

ha'penny of his money, and it's not for me the police should be
coming to this house.

CHAVASSE: Be quiet, Mary!

MARY: Quiet is it, and you slandering and laying false charges on
my character. I'll not be quiet! It's to silence me he would have
me in jail!

CAREY: Be easy, woman, in the presence of the dead. I'll be coming to have a talk with you another time.

MARY (*shouting*): And if she's dead who killed her? Answer me
that. It's him! He did it! And now he'd have me in prison to
stop my mouth.

CHAVASSE: Get out of here, Mary!

MARY: I'm going all right. But I'm not going to jail without first
telling them how the Mistress came by her death. Murder! Murder!

CAREY: See here, my woman, I was going to deal leniently with
you the way the Doctor asked me, but if you're not careful
you'll be adding another charge to the list, and that for public
slander and insulting behaviour. You can't go around making
charges like that against respectable people.

MARY: And who says he's respectable? I tell you I know a thing
or two. I've seen what's going on and I tell you he murdered
her.

CAREY: Ah, you're mad, woman. What call would the like of Dr.
Chavasse have for murdering his wife? I'll leave you now, before you rile me into running you in, Doctor or no Doctor. (*He
turns to go*)

CHAVASSE: Will you calm down, Mary, and nobody will harm you.

CAREY: Good day, sir. Good day, Dr. Hollingshead. If you have
any more trouble with this woman just let me know. You'll
certify the death in the usual way, I suppose?

CHAVASSE: Yes, Sergeant. Dr. Hollingshead will do so. (ANICE
gives a start, but remains silent)

CAREY: That will be all right, sir. (*To* MARY) And let you look to
your tongue, for you've not heard the last of this, my girl.

MARY: And well might she certify the death and she his fancy woman! Do you not know what's between them two, John Carey?

CHAVASSE: Mary!

CAREY (*pausing in the doorway with a new interest*): What's that you're saying?

MARY: Why wouldn't he murder her and the two of them breaking the law of God and man to the scandal of a Christian country! Ask them what happened last December year. Ask them that, and if they won't tell you 'tis myself that'll put you wise. Why wouldn't he murder her and that black sin on their souls?

CAREY: Mary Quirke, this is a serious charge you're making.

CHAVASSE: Get out of here, you foul-mouthed bitch, before I throw you out!

MARY: I'll stand by it. Every word of it. And if you want proof, let you look in the locked drawer of that desk. There's papers in there that'll open your eyes, John Carey.

CHAVASSE: Mary, I swear I'll . . .

CAREY: One moment, Doctor, if you please. How do you know what's in a locked drawer, Mary Quirke?

MARY: Never mind how I know. There's ways of knowing when you've lived a year or two in a house. If you don't believe me, look for yourself, and then call me a liar!

(*There is a pause, and then* CAREY *comes slowly over to the desk, where he tries the drawer*)

CAREY (*suspiciously*): Dr. Chavasse, I'm sorry to trouble you, sir. But would you have any objection to letting me have a look in this drawer?

Curtain

SCENE 2

A month later. The antechamber to the Law Library in the Four Courts, Dublin. To the right are glazed swing doors on the far side of which a Crier sits at a high desk. From time to time, as they are asked for by the Solicitors in the antechamber, he calls out the names of the Barristers within. The Barristers then emerge from the Library and consult with their Solicitors or pass to and fro on their way to the various Courts. To the left is a small boy with a table and benches for consultations.

CRIER: Patrick Moo—er! Arthur Pea—cock!

(ANICE *enters right with* ROCHE, *a solicitor*)

ROCHE: Just wait here a moment while I call Mr. Thin. (*He goes towards the Crier's desk*)

1ST ATTORNEY: I say, do you know who that is? Anice Hollingshead.

2ND ATTORNEY: Isn't that the woman in the Chavasse murder?

1ST ATTORNEY: The very one.

2ND ATTORNEY: Um. Looks just what I'd have expected.

CRIER: Theo—bald Thin!

3RD ATTORNEY: What did you expect? Is there something behind that case?

2ND ATTORNEY: Of course there is. I know some of the local people, and the place is full of rumours.

CRIER: Tee Jay . . . Wright!

1ST ATTORNEY: There's Thin talking to Roche. Isn't he Counsel for the prisoner?

2ND ATTORNEY: Yes, God help him!

3RD ATTORNEY: God help who?

2ND ATTORNEY: The prisoner, of course. (*They all laugh*) I think I'd rather plead guilty myself. (*They part, still laughing*)

ROCHE: This is the Doctor's Counsel, Mr. Thin. Dr. Hollingshead.

ANICE: How do you do?

THIN (*a cross-grained, self-important little man*): Yes, yes, good day, Miss Hollingshead. I sent for you before the hearing, although I don't usually approve of interviewing witnesses. A practice that leads to abuse.

ROCHE: But this is rather a special case, Mr. Thin, don't you think?

THIN: Yes. A very difficult case. Very tricky. We shall need all our wits about us.

ROCHE: Indeed. Indeed.

ANICE: Oh, but why? Surely you don't think there's any real danger of the case going against Dr. Chavasse?

THIN: Who can tell? Who can tell? However, we must all hope for the best.

ROCHE: Indeed you may be sure that Dr. Chavasse's case will be in good hands. The very best will be done for him.

THIN: Thank you, Roche, for your good opinion. But we had better keep these testimonials for another occasion.

CRIER: Sm—iiiiith!

ANICE: But this is unthinkable! He's an innocent man. You can't mean . . .

THIN: Now, my dear young lady, I must ask you not to raise your voice. Let us cross each brook in turn, as we come to it. I have one or two difficulties that I wish to clear up, and I must ask you, please, to keep your head. It is a very serious matter.

ROCHE: Come, come, Doctor. We can rely on you, I trust.

ANICE: I'm sorry, Mr. Thin. But for a moment you took me aback. I had no idea that . . . I promise to do my best.

THIN: Much better. Much better. Now all I want you to do is to listen carefully to what I am saying and to answer my questions briefly and as truthfully as possible.

ROCHE: Yes, Dr. Hollingshead. Please concentrate on what Mr. Thin is saying.

THIN: And perhaps you also will be kind enough to keep quiet, Roche.

ANICE: Well, what is it you want to know?

THIN: In the first place, without wishing in any way to throw doubts upon the *bona fides* of Dr. Chavasse, I do think that both his conduct and your own after the—er—death leave much to be desired.

ANICE: What do you mean?

THIN: It is unfortunate . . . most unfortunate, that there should have been any attempt to conceal the real cause of death. The death certificate that you were proposing to give . . .

ANICE: But . . .

THIN: Most regrettable . . . very embarrassing.

ROCHE: Ttt-ttt-ttt.

ANICE: But I never gave any certificate. I never even . . .

THIN: You were going to.

ANICE: No, I wasn't.

THIN: My dear Miss Hollingshead, please understand that in a matter such as this, there must be absolute candour between counsel and witness. Let us have no quibbling.

ANICE: But I'm not quibbling.

THIN: You heard the Doctor tell the Sergeant that Mrs. Chavasse had died from gastro-enteritis?

ANICE: No. I was in the next room when he said that.

THIN: Please. It comes to the same thing. You knew that he had or was going to say so.

ANICE: Yes. I'm not trying to . . .

THIN: And you did not contradict him when he told the Sergeant that you would give the certificate.

ANICE: But what could I do? If I had said anything . . .

THIN (*in a louder tone*): You did not contradict him. Let us have that quite clear.

ANICE: Why do you keep on at me like this? You talk as though you were trying to prove us guilty . . . as thought you thought . . .

ROCHE: Oh, come, come. This is most . . .

THIN (*after crushing* ROCHE *with a glance*): My dear young lady, it is not part of my professional duties to reach any conclusion on such a point. I am trying to make the best case that I can for Dr. Chavasse under very difficult circumstances . . . very difficult circumstances.

ROCHE: Yes, indeed, Doctor Hollingshead. You musn't talk like that to Mr. Thin. You must trust him to know what is best.

CRIER: Michael O——Sullivan!

THIN: Will you kindly not interrupt, Roche.

ANICE: I do trust Mr. Thin. It's just that I can't see . . .

THIN (*holding up a hand*): Were I convinced in my own mind of Dr. Chavasse's guilt I would still defend him to the best of my ability. It is his right, and those are the demands of my profession. But I could not state his case with the same conviction and enthusiasm. I admit it frankly, Miss Hollingshead. That is why it is your duty to clear up as far as possible all these questions that are troubling me. You must keep nothing back.

ANICE: Yes, Mr. Thin. I understand, and I shall try to do my best. I admit that he had the idea that I might help him to hush it up. It was foolish I know.

THIN (*nodding solemnly*): Exceedingly foolish.

ROCHE (*following his example*): Ttt-ttt-ttt.

THIN: Please do not make those irritating noises, Roche. And now, Miss Hollingshead, perhaps you will tell me what was the object in trying to conceal the true facts?

ANICE: He didn't want it to be known that she had committed suicide.

THIN: Why not?

ANICE: Obviously no one likes such a thing to happen in one's family. She was an exceedingly neurotic woman, and for some time had been becoming steadily worse. At least, so I have been told. I never saw her myself, professionally.

THIN: And to what was this . . . er degeneration attributable?

ROCHE: Yes, what, Doctor?

THIN: Hush!

ANICE: I have told you. It was something psychological. She had suicidal tendencies.

THIN: Miss Hollingshead, you are still not being candid with me. There was some reason for this suicide, if it was suicide. And it is the same reason that inspired you both to make this unfortunate attempt to avoid a post-mortem. Even neurotics must have some occasion, however fantastic, for suicide.

ANICE: You know quite well what the reason was. But as you insist on my putting it into words, I suppose I must. She was obsessed with the idea that Dr. Chavasse was having an affair with me. (*The two men nod significantly*)

THIN: Now we are getting somewhere.

ANICE: But it isn't true, I tell you. Until he sent for me on the day she died I hadn't spoken to him for eighteen months. I swear it. Anybody will bear me out. They can't prove anything to the contrary. She was wrong, I tell you.

THIN: But those letters that were found in the desk . . . surely . . .

ANICE: They were old ones he should never have kept. Oh, I don't deny we were once in love. But that was all over and done with.

THIN: Ah. So that the allegations of the servant, Mary Quirke, are true?

ANICE: No, no, I tell you. That was all spite and venom. Nobody could believe her. She's a thief. Frank had sent for the police to have her arrested.

THIN: Please, please. That is not what I asked you.

CRIER: Henry—Harrican!

ANICE: I don't care, but it's the truth.

ROCHE: Come, come. This is no place for these exhibitions.

THIN: And will you kindly not interfere, Roche, when I am attempting to concentrate. I see the State Solicitor over there. I wish to speak to him about this case, and I hope when I return that I shall find that you have pulled yourself together, Miss Hollingshead. (*He rises and crosses to* POER *who is standing by the swing doors, where they are presently joined by* HARRICAN)

ROCHE: Now, Doctor, see what you've done. You've annoyed him.

ANICE: Don't you try to bully me too. I'm not a criminal.

ROCHE: I think you scarcely realize what a serious position we are in.

ANICE: What right have you to talk like that! It's Frank and I who are in a serious position. Not you or Mr. Thin. It's we who have cause to be annoyed.

ROCHE: There, there. We must keep calm.

ANICE: Then please stop telling me to be serious. (HARRICAN's *laugh booms out*)

CRIER: Herbert Winter! George O . . . Brennan!

ANICE: There's that man, Poer. Ever since this dreadful business started he has hounded us from pillar to post. He's the one at the back of it all, though God knows what we ever did to him. What are they joking about? It's not so funny for us.

ROCHE: Oh, Poer's not so bad. He's always ready to be accommodating.

ANICE: Very nice, I'm sure. But it's we, poor creatures, who are on the rack, while you gentlemen accommodate each other.

ROCHE: Oh, come now. Isn't that a characteristic of all professions? You should understand, Doctor. How else could we carry on?

ANICE: Perhaps you're right. All the same I can't help finding it a little galling to be told to calm down, while our counsel goes away for a few minutes' friendly chat with the other side.

ROCHE: My dear lady, it's a common fallacy amongst lay clients that opposing counsel ought never to speak to each other. Now I ask you, is that reasonable?

ANICE: I know I'm unstrung. Give me a moment or two and I shall be all right again.

ROCHE: That's better. Much better.

4TH ATTORNEY: That's Anice Hollingshead. They say she's going to be arrested too.

5TH ATTORNEY: A curious case. I hear the wife used to drink and beat the child.

HARRICAN: In five minutes, Poer.

POER: Right. I'll come back. (HARRICAN *goes back into the library and* POER *goes off in the opposite direction, while* THIN *returns to the table*)

CRIER (*in answer to the telephone bell*): Come in. Try the Father Matthew Hall. There's a prior mortgage on him.

THIN: Well, perhaps we may continue.

ANICE: I'm sorry for losing control of myself. I'll tell you all there is to tell about my relations with Dr. Chavasse if you wish it.

THIN: Perhaps that would be best.

ANICE: We were lovers. It began two years ago or more during the typhus epidemic. We were together on Inishfree. He was very gallant, and was literally working himself to death. He is like that, you know, where his job is concerned. I couldn't help admiring him.

THIN: You knew, of course, that he was a married man?

ANICE: Yes, I knew. But I thought he was—oh, I'm not going to excuse myself. Yes, I knew he was married, but it didn't seem to matter. I suppose we both needed each other at the time, and one thing led to another.

THIN: I see.

ANICE: When I found out that . . . when we knew what was going to happen, we intended at first to go away together. We didn't know each other so well then as we do now. I don't believe we could ever have done it.

THIN: So you fell back upon another—er—expedient?

ANICE: No. It's a lie, what that woman tells of us! The worst, dirtiest kind of lie, because it wraps up in a falsehood something that is half true. We didn't do what she said we did. I don't say we wouldn't have, but we didn't.

THIN: You mean with regard to the—er—child?

ANICE: Yes. With regard to that. You see, I was very upset at the time, and as it turned out . . .

THIN: Yes?

ANICE: It wasn't . . . necessary.

THIN: I see.

ANICE: There! That's the whole truth, and you see the kind of beastly lie she has made out of it. We parted after that. It was all hopeless. I'd have gone away if I could have found another job. As it was, we swore we'd never see each other again. Nor did we . . . to speak. Not until the day she died.

THIN: How much of this did Mrs. Chavasse know?

ANICE: I can't tell. It came as a shock to me to find that she knew at all. I had imagined that it was all over and done with, but I was living in a fool's paradise, I'm afraid.

THIN: You think that Chavasse told her?

ANICE: I'm sure he didn't. But he would never have been able to deceive her, once she started to suspect anything. Mary Quirke is at the bottom of her finding out. I'm sure of it. She managed somehow to get at those letters. Oh, he was a fool to have kept them!

THIN: Yes, a very difficult case.

ROCHE (*his eyes shining*): Oh, indeed!

ANICE: We were wrong from the start in trying to hush anything up. It never pays in the long run. But thank God, it's all out now. I've nothing to conceal any longer.

THIN: My dear young lady, it is very far from being all out yet, in spite of Mary Quirke's statement. And you may be quite sure that I shall take every precaution to keep it out at the trial.

ROCHE: By all means. By all means.

THIN: Sssh!

ANICE: But you're not going on trying to conceal the truth?

THIN: Most certainly I am. When you have reached my years of experience, Miss Hollingshead, you will realize that where sex is concerned it is always best to conceal everything—the truth most of all. That is never believed. At all costs we must keep sex out of this case.

ROCHE: Anything else. But not sex.

ANICE: I don't believe I can lie about it any more. When they start questioning me I don't know what I'll say.

THIN: Never fear, Miss Hollingshead. We won't call you as a witness at all until we have succeeded in excluding this aspect of the case.

ANICE: Then I may not have to give evidence? Oh, thank God!

THIN: Purely medical evidence maybe. But we won't risk it until we have won the case on the other points and are comparatively safe.

ANICE: But how can you keep it out if the other side call that woman Quirke as a witness?

THIN: I shall make it my business to object strenuously to all evidence that is not legally relevant.

ANICE: Surely if you can show them the kind of woman she is . . . once they know why she started all this against Frank . . . that he had sent for the police . . .

THIN: No, Miss Hollingshead, we will not do anything of the sort. Please let that be understood.

ANICE: But why not?

THIN: For legal reasons which you may safely leave to me. Please just do as I say and don't bother yourself with the law of evidence. Nothing must be said against Quirke and you may rest assured that I am taking the proper course in so advising you.

ROCHE: Quite.

ANICE: If they believe her, I can't see why they aren't prosecuting me as well as Frank. I must be just as guilty, if not of murder, at least of the other thing.

THIN: Well, you know Miss Hollingshead, the letters are rather ambiguous, and I think you may assume without some further corroboration they will scarcely move against you for . . . er . . . illegal practices on the sole evidence of Mary Quirke. As an accessory to the murder charge . . . possibly, in the event of Chavasse being convicted. That remains to be seen. But for the other, no. I think decidedly not. (POER *comes back to the library door*)

ANICE: I see.

CRIER: Henery Harr—ican!

THIN: Well that, I think, is all.

ANICE: Mr. Thin, I realize all that you are doing for us. If there is anything else that I can do to help . . .

THIN (*rising*): Nothing, Miss Hollingshead. Nothing. Except to rely upon me to know what is best, and to follow my instructions to the letter. And now good morning. We will meet again on Wednesday at the trial. (*He goes into the library as* HARRICAN *emerges*)

1ST COUNSEL: Sure they all drink down there.

2ND COUNSEL: Well, what would you expect? Think of the Eskimos.

POER (*coming to the table with* HARRICAN): Well, Roche. Oh, how do you do, Doctor Hollingshead? We meet again. (*She sweeps out past him*)

POER: Well, well. Your witness, I think, Roche. She doesn't seem to want to do herself any good.

ROCHE: Don't mind her, Liam. She thinks you're going after her next. Are you, by the way?

POER: You'd like to know, wouldn't you? See you later. (ROCHE *goes out*)

CRIER: Michael Thom—pson!

HARRICAN: Well Poer, still the same big failure with the ladies, I see. (*His laugh booms out*)

POER: I'm afraid you rather flatter Doctor Hollingshead with such a title. After you've read the depositions you'll probably agree with me.

HARRICAN: My dear fellow, why must you always assume that counsel has never read any of your precious documents?

POER: Oh, I admit that you often turn them over, and make a few pencil marks at inappropriate places. But you can't deceive us that way in the State Solicitor's Office.

HARRICAN (*turning over the papers*): Believe me, we treat these dossiers of irrelevancies with a great deal more respect than they usually deserve. Well, what have we here? The same old useless farrago. A map of the house—list of the contents of the dispensing room—photograph of the local parish priest—statements—statements—letters—statements. Tell me, Poer, are the guards paid by the folio or do they turn out this kind of thing just for the love of it?

POER: You can be very facetious, I know. But how can they tell what turn a case like this will take, once it gets into the hands of you gentlemen of the Bar?

HARRICAN: Well, well. The corpse's finger-prints! Isn't that interesting! And I imagined that this was a poisoning charge! Do you think you could manage to work in a model steam-engine somewhere? I promised my small son that on the first opportunity . . .

POER: What I want you to look at is the pathologist's report.

HARRICAN: Who? What? Oh, this thing. Who's this O'Something anyway? Never heard of him before.

POER: He's the new assistant. I'm told he's quite efficient.

HARRICAN: Officious, you mean. I see that he finds that Mrs. Chavasse was murdered. Who the devil asked him that?

POER: Yes, I know that he goes much too far. He's young, and I suppose, anxious to show off. But you can see what he means if you read it through.

HARRICAN: No need for a trial at all when we have Mr. O'Quilt to settle it all for us. Um. Sinacidic poisoning. And the defence—suicide. You know, Poer, we'll never get a conviction in this case.

POER: Don't you think so?

HARRICAN: My dear fellow, not if we had half a million exhibits. The whole thing is far too much in the air. It's all spite and speculation. There's no motive for the jury.

POER: Good God, no motive! And the fellow having lived in adultery with another woman! Do you mean to tell me, you don't believe that he did it?

HARRICAN: Of course I believe that he did it. I am always prepared to believe that any husband has contemplated murdering his wife. I am a married man myself.

POER: Ah, for God's sake, stop being funny.

HARRICAN: Why shouldn't I be funny? I have no animus against the poor fellow. He may poison half a dozen wives and welcome for all I care. But what I do say is this. If you want me to get a conviction you'll have to stop sending me these damned supplementary briefs and all these tomfool exhibits and give me some evidence of a reasonable motive.

POER: Haven't you got Mary Quirke's deposition?

HARRICAN: Pooh. Mere evidence of bad character. From a worse character, as far as I can see.

POER: It's corroborated to some extent by the letters in the drawer.

HARRICAN: A lot of stale rubbish! What of it? The fellow procured an abortion for Hollingshead nearly two years ago. Suppose he did. That doesn't prove he murdered his wife last month. I tell you, Poer, those letters won't even be admitted as evidence, any more than Quirke's deposition will.

POER: But surely it's relevant? Doesn't it all go to show the circumstances?

HARRICAN: The circumstances a couple of years ago. Oh, I'll try it on, of course, but you know what Drooley is. Anything he can keep from the jury, he'll keep from the jury. There's nothing he likes better than an opportunity for treating them all as half-wits, which God knows they will be. No. Unless we can show that they've been at it since then, it's five to one that Drooley will rule out both the deposition and the letters.

POER: I've done my best about that, but I haven't been able to find out anything else so far.

HARRICAN: Then in my opinion Mary Quirke is a washout. In any event she ought to be in jail herself.

POER: You'd be surprised how much of the evidence we work on comes from people who ought to be in jail themselves. But it seems to do its job all the same.

HARRICAN: Oh, once we get the love interest to the jury, it'll be believed all right. And anything else we like to suggest along with it. Never fear about that. They always believe the dirt once it starts flying. But the jury will never hear about it as it stands.

POER: Well, all I say is, damn the rules of evidence. I can see what you mean about Quirke's deposition, but it's a damned scandal if we aren't going to be allowed to show the whole truth. But wait a minute. Suppose they attack her character in cross-examination? Couldn't we get it in then, in reply, as evidence of *his* bad character?

HARRICAN: Oh, if they did that, of course we'd have them. But there's not a hope in hell, my dear fellow. They'll lay off Quirke, you may be sure.

POER: It'll be a great temptation to them.

HARRICAN: Not to Thin. For all his damn pomposity, Thin knows his stuff.

POER: Yes. He's no fool I admit. By the way, do you want me to subpoena Anice Hollingshead?

HARRICAN: No. Leave it to Thin to call her, so that I can cross-examine. She's no use to us as our witness. Well, there you have it all. A nice little bit of tactics. But in my opinion, if this is all the case you can give me, there'll be an acquittal. In the meantime I want my lunch, which is far more important. (*He goes off with a breezy nod*)

Curtain

ACT TWO

ACT TWO

The Central Criminal Court, a few days later. (SERGEANT CAREY *is in the witness box under examination by* HARRICAN, *who exhibits all the bluff, good-humoured indifference of counsel who feels that his case is a hopeless one*)

CAREY: From the door to the fireplace, eighteen foot ten. From the window to the door, twenty-one foot six. From the fireplace to the couch on which I found the body, seven foot ten. From the couch on which I found the body to the window . . .

JUDGE (*writing*): Seven feet ten inches. Just one moment, Sergeant. Tell me, Mr. Harrican, do you attach much significance to these measurements?

HARRICAN: None whatever, melud. I am quite ready to pass them over, unless my learned friend insists.

THIN: Melud, I don't see that the exact position of the body is a matter of any great importance. (THIN, *in contradistinction to* HARRICAN, *is sharp, intense, and on his toes all the time*)

JUDGE: I think then that we may take the measurements as admitted.

HARRICAN: Thank you, melud. I appreciate Your Lordship's kindness and also that of my learned friend. And now, Sergeant, briefly what else do you produce?

CAREY: I produce a list of the contents of the dispensing room . . . extract taken from the Poison Book of Mr. Theodore Doyle, Pharmaceutical Chemist of No. 12 Wolfe Tone Street . . . set of finger prints taken from the deceased . . . set of finger prints taken from the accused . . . and a bundle of nine letters taken by me from a drawer in the hall on the day of the death after duly obtaining a search warrant.

HARRICAN: Hand them in.

JUDGE: Mark them all, Mr. Curran. (*As the* REGISTRAR *takes them* THIN *leaps to his feet, quivering*)

HARRICAN (*blandly*): Does my learned friend wish to intervene?

THIN: Melud, I object to the admission of these letters. They have no bearing on the present charge.

HARRICAN: Melud, the relevance of the letters will appear later when we come to the evidence of the accused's servant, Mary Quirke, who . . .

THIN: Evidence which my learned friend knows perfectly well I intend to object to.

HARRICAN: I was about to add, melud, before I was interrupted, that on the remand my learned friend objected to a portion of this witness's evidence . . . the portion marked 'A' in her deposition, melud . . . and it was only admitted by the District Justice subject to whatever ruling Your Lordship might make on it at the trial.

JUDGE: Let me see. The portion marked 'A'. Whose deposition, did you say?

HARRICAN: The deposition of Mary Quirke, melud.

THIN: Your Lordship will see that I consider it vital to my case that the portion marked 'A' should be excluded as irrelevant and embarrassing. That is why I ventured to interrupt my learned friend.

JUDGE: Mary Quirke. Let me see, now.

HARRICAN: You can be quite sure, Mr. Thin, that I had no intention of going into any disputed part of the evidence before His Lordship has had an opportunity of ruling upon it.

JUDGE: Ah, here we are, I think. The portion marked 'A'.

HARRICAN: I'm sorry if you think that I would have tried . . .

THIN: Oh, not at all, not at all. I never wished to suggest that you would, Mr. Harrican.

JUDGE: Just one moment, Mr. Thin, if you please, while I read the portion marked 'A'. (*After a significant pause*) Ah . . . um . . . I have now read the portion marked 'A' and I think that I appreciate your objection to its going to the jury. I am quite sure that Mr. Harrican had no intention of doing anything improper without permission from me.

HARRICAN: Indeed melud, I'd be very loath to do anything improper even with Your Lordship's permission.

JUDGE: Ah. Quite so. It seems to me that the best time to go into this matter, if it is to be gone into at all, is when Mary Quirke is called as a witness. You intend to press for its admission, Mr. Harrican?

HARRICAN: I do indeed, melud. I was just about to propose what Your Lordship has been good enough to suggest.

THIN: I agree entirely. I apologize for interrupting.

HARRICAN: Not at all my dear fellow. It's a pleasure.

JUDGE: Then we will leave the admissibility of these letters until later on. Does that conclude your examination, Mr. Harrican, or has the Sergeant got anything else to put in?

HARRICAN: That's all, melud, I'm glad to say.

JUDGE: Yes, Mr. Thin?

THIN: I have nothing to add, melud.

JUDGE: Just one thing before you go, Sergeant. I have been looking at this list you took of the contents of the dispensing room, and very painstaking you have been, I must say. I notice, however, that there is no mention of Sinacide anywhere in the list. Is that correct?

CAREY: Yes, My Lord. All that was there is put down.

JUDGE: I see. You searched the rest of the house?

CAREY: Yes, My Lord. But I could find nothing else in the way of drugs.

JUDGE: Curious. Thank you, Sergeant. (*He comes out of the witness box*)

HARRICAN: Dominick Mapother!

REGISTRAR: Dominick Mapother! (MAPOTHER *enters the box*)

REGISTRAR: Raise the book in your right hand. I swear by Almighty God . . . (MAPOTHER *smiles politely*)

REGISTRAR: I swear by Almighty God . . .

MAPOTHER: Yes, my dear sir.

REGISTRAR: Repeat after me, please, I swear by Almighty God.

MAPOTHER: Yes, my dear sir, I swear by Almighty God.

REGISTRAR: That the evidence I shall give in this case to the Court and jury.

MAPOTHER: That the evidence I shall give in this case to the Court and jury.

REGISTRAR: Shall be the truth the whole truth.

MAPOTHER: Yes, shall be the truth the whole truth.

REGISTRAR: And nothing but the truth what's your name?

MAPOTHER: And nothing but the truth what's my name. Dominick Mapother, my dear sir. M . . . Ah . . . P . . . O . . . T . . . Haitch . . . E . . . R. An unusual and difficult name.

REGISTRAR: Dominick Mapother melud.

HARRICAN: Where do you live, my good man?

MAPOTHER: I live in my old Grannie's house at the corner of the Ashdown Road may God long preserve her.

HARRICAN: Now speak up, my good man, so that all these gentlemen in the jury box can hear you.

MAPOTHER: There is nothing I wouldn't have them hear, my dear sir. They are all decent men the like of myself.

HARRICAN: What's your business?

MAPOTHER: My business amongst those present or my business in this Vale of Tears?

HARRICAN: How do you make your living?

MAPOTHER: Ah, my dear sir, it's a poor living one can make in a discouraging world. Times is hard indeed for the lowly. I had a cow once, but she died, the poor beast, and that's the truth of it.

HARRICAN: From which I take it, you are either a farmer or a cattle dealer?

MAPOTHER: Incorrect, my dear sir. For how can a man be a farmer without a farm or a dealer without a cow? Not mind you that I mightn't have included myself in one or other category in the days of my pride before I was brought low by the lamented demise of my unfortunate cow.

THIN: I object to this evidence.

HARRICAN: Oh, come, come.

JUDGE: There is something in Mr. Thin's objection, I think. I am sure that we all have the deepest sympathy with this gentleman over the loss of his . . . er . . . ruminant.

MAPOTHER: I thank you, my dear Lord.

JUDGE: But the fact remains, it is not the death of his cow that we are investigating here.

HARRICAN: I am grateful for Your Lordship's ruling. I think we may pass over the question of this witness's occupation. Tell me, my man, have you known Dr. Chavasse for long?

MAPOTHER: Ten years, my good sir. Oh, a fine man, but what a fall! What a come down!

HARRICAN: You were in Dr. Chavasse's house the morning his wife died?

MAPOTHER: I was indeed. I was there in person sitting in the waiting-room just off the hall, when lo, the whole painful episode was unfolded before me.

HARRICAN: What brought you there?

MAPOTHER: I was hoping you would ask me that question. You see, sir, I had a cow . . . a noble work of nature, both meat and drink to rich and poor alike.

JUDGE: It seems, Mr. Harrican, that we are back on the subject of this cow again.

HARRICAN: A most insinuating animal it would appear, melud.

JUDGE: I have noticed before that in the most hard-fought actions in these courts a cow almost invariably appears. (*Polite laughter in court*)

HARRICAN: Come now, Mapother. Never mind the cow. Tell us what you saw at Dr. Chavasse's.

MAPOTHER: I saw nothing, my dear sir, being in the adjoining room. All that I did was to hear.

HARRICAN: And what did you hear?

MAPOTHER: I heard him administer the coo de grass—the death blow. Oh, my dear sir, a shocking experience. A mortifying exhibition of human fraylity.

THIN: I object. This is not evidence. Let him tell what happened and leave it at that.

JUDGE: Yes, Mr. Harrican. It seems to me that, picturesque as your witness is in his description, it is for us to determine whether there was anything in the nature of a . . . er . . . coo de grass. (*Renewed laughter*)

HARRICAN: Quite so, melud. From coos back to cows is only a short step. I shall put it to the witness another way. Who did you see when you arrived?

MAPOTHER: Well, first I saw Miss Quirke. You see, sir, my straits were very pressing and Miss Quirke remarked to me . . .

HARRICAN: You mustn't tell us what she said.

MAPOTHER: Really? Is that not allowed?

HARRICAN: No. Simply tell us what you did.

MAPOTHER: I beg your pardon, my dear sir. Well, I went and waited in the waiting-room. Hence the name.

HARRICAN: For the Doctor to come in?

MAPOTHER: Exactly. You have summed up the situation precisely. I had been promised a bottle of medicine for my unfortunate . . .

HARRICAN: If it was for the cow never mind. Well?

MAPOTHER: Well, I suppose I was sitting there for a short space of time immersed in gloomy speculations on the minor problems of life, when I thought I heard voices raised in the hall. So rising to my feet I emerged from my retirement and approached the room where poor Mrs. Chavasse lay stretched in her agony.

HARRICAN: How did you know she was there?

MAPOTHER: Well, my dear sir, that unfortunately is one of the things I must not tell you, for it is what Miss Quirke said when I first came in.

HARRICAN: And could you hear what was going on in the next room?

MAPOTHER: I could hear, sir, did I choose to listen. But not being of an eavesdropping turn of mind I would consider it beneath me to make a point of listening.

HARRICAN: Quite so. You didn't listen. Now tell us what you heard.

MAPOTHER: I will sir, indeed. I heard the Doctor say to the lady, 'It's now or never.' 'Keep this quiet for God's sake,' he says. And then Miss Hollingshead asked him what he had given the unfortunate woman and he said that he had stuck a needle in her heart about an hour before. Oh, a very discreditable scene it was, though, mind you, the full horror of it didn't dawn on me till I went home and I found . . .

HARRICAN: Is that all you heard?

MAPOTHER: That's all, sir, except for the lady saying he could leave it and there was nothing more to be done for the poor woman was dead R.I.P. Then Dr. Chavasse comes out and knocks into me, and, my good sir, I regret to have to say he used expressions strictly unparliamentary which I would not care to repeat even to you, sir.

HARRICAN: And then you went away?

MAPOTHER: I did, sir. Me and the child. We were ordered out of the house hardly waiting to mention the subject of my visit. We were one and all more upset than I can say, but it was not till after I had got home that I realized for the first time how false a friend a man could be. My cow . . .

JUDGE: Please, Mr. Mapother, do not mention that beast again.

HARRICAN: That will do, my good man. (*He sits down*)

MAPOTHER: Is that all I have to say?

THIN: No, sir. I have some questions to put to you. And I want you if possible to answer them directly, and forget for a few minutes all irrelevant matters.

MAPOTHER: Yes, sir. I'm only trying to do my best, and to tell the truth and the whole truth as I swore to this gentleman, the half-Judge here. (*He indicates the* REGISTRAR)

THIN: You seem to be very venomous against Dr. Chavasse.

MAPOTHER: Not venomous, my dear sir. Merely pained. Deeply pained. I would never have thought it of such a man.

THIN: He was a good friend of yours once?

MAPOTHER: Oh, the best of friends. Many a kindly thought.

THIN: Then may I ask what is it that has turned you against him?

MAPOTHER: His treatment of suffering living creatures. His callous and heartless behaviour.

THIN: With regard to his wife?

MAPOTHER: Yes, my dear sir. That and other things.

THIN: What other things?

MAPOTHER: My dear sir, much as I would like to, I cannot tell you that.

THIN: And why not, pray?

MAPOTHER: Because I have been requested by my Dear Lordship here never to mention my unfortunate cow again.

THIN: Very well, very well. Leave it at that. But just tell me this, Mapother. When you were in the house did you hear any sounds suggestive of a struggle in the adjoining room?

MAPOTHER: Oh, no, sir.

THIN: You didn't hear Mrs. Chavasse cry or call out? Or make any sounds of protest?

MAPOTHER: None, my dear sir. It was a peaceful end, God help the poor soul.

THIN: And I put it to you that had there been any kind of a struggle or protest from Mrs. Chavasse before she died, you would have heard it?

MAPOTHER: Such would have been my lot. Not that I was listening, you will understand.

THIN: That is as it may be. Now you remember what you heard the two doctors say to each other?

MAPOTHER: Till my dying day, my dear sir.

THIN: Might not they have said everything that you heard, in the course of their efforts to revive Mrs. Chavasse?

HARRICAN: With the greatest regard for my learned friend, I must object to such a question. That is a conclusion for the Court to draw.

JUDGE: Yes, I think that is scarcely a proper question for the present witness.

THIN: Then melud, if I am not allowed to pursue this line of country I must respectfully resume my seat.

JUDGE: I take it, Mr. Thin, that you wish me to note your objection to my ruling?

THIN: If Your Lordship pleases. So long as it is on the notes I am satisfied.

JUDGE: Come, come, Mr. Thin. This has been a most amicable trial up to the present. I hope that it will continue so.

THIN: Believe me, melud, nobody has derived greater pleasure from it up to the present than I have.

JUDGE: And I am sure our friend, Mr. Harrican's, sentiments are the same. Come. Let us proceed.

HARRICAN: By all means, melud. I call Seamus Ua Caoilte.

JUDGE (*as the latter comes to the witness box*): Is this your expert witness, Mr. Harrican?

HARRICAN: It is, melud. The State Pathologist.

JUDGE (*to the* JURY): Indeed. We must listen to this, gentlemen, with particular attention.

MAPOTHER: Is that all?

HARRICAN: Yes, yes. Stand down, my man.

MAPOTHER: Well now, my dear sir, with regard to my professional expenses . . .

HARRICAN: That's all right. We'll go into that later.

MAPOTHER: First there will be travelling expenses. And then there is the cost of living in the City . . . Oh, very high, my dear sir, as we all know. Not to mention general expenses.

HARRICAN: What might they be?

MAPOTHER: Payment in respect of all the work I might have been doing in the meantime.

JUDGE: What is all this, Mr. Harrican?

HARRICAN: It appears, melud, that Mr. Mapother's extensive business activities have been interfered with.

JUDGE: Then let him hurry back to them at once. Take him away, somebody, and let us proceed.

UA CAOILTE (*a priggish-looking young man in pince-nez, after gabbling the oath*): Seamus Ua Caoilte.

JUDGE: What name did you say?

UA CAOILTE: Ua Caoilte, My Lord.

JUDGE: Eh, what?

HARRICAN: Little, melud.

JUDGE: Oh, I see.

HARRICAN: You are the State Pathologist?

UA CAOILTE: I am the Assistant State Pathologist.

HARRICAN: Quite so. In the course of your duties did you examine the body of Mrs. Chavasse?

UA CAOILTE: I did.

HARRICAN: Did you reach any conclusions as to the cause of her death?

UA CAOILTE: I had no difficulty whatever in diagnosing the cause of death. It was a simple case. One of the simplest in my experience.

HARRICAN: And what did Mrs. Chavasse die of?

UA CAOILTE: She died of Sinacidic poisoning.

HARRICAN: And you embodied your findings in this report?

UA CAOILTE: That is correct.

HARRICAN: I hand in a copy, melud. And one for the jury as well. Now Mr. Ua Caoilte, just let us go through this report in detail . . .

THIN: Melud—excuse me interrupting—

HARRICAN: Not at all. I like it.

THIN: Melud, I strongly object to this report.

JUDGE: Dear me. On what grounds, Mr. Thin?

THIN: On the ground that Mr. Ua Caoilte has overstepped the bounds of his duties as State Pathologist. The purpose of this trial is to determine the guilt or innocence of my client. Yet I find that this so-called expert has presumed to state in his report not merely that Mrs. Chavasse died from the effects of Sinacidic acid, but that she was murdered.

HARRICAN (*with insincere gravity*): Melud, I really must take exception to the language of my learned friend. To refer to the Assistant State Pathologist as a 'so-called expert' is more than I can allow to pass.

THIN: Kindly do not interrupt, Mr. Harrican.

HARRICAN: I certainly will interrupt. I ask the protection of the Court for my witness.

JUDGE: Yes, Mr. Thin, you do seem to have couched your objection in somewhat violent terms, however legitimate it may be.

THIN: Melud, if I have done so, it is not without justification. It is the function of the State Expert to determine the cause of death and no more. What right has he to attempt to prejudice the issue in this scandalous way? Melud, I will go further and say that this report so far oversteps the bounds of what is right and proper in the circumstances as to amount to Contempt of Court.

HARRICAN (*blandly*): I really cannot let this pass. I must insist upon my learned friend withdrawing his opprobrious expression, 'so-called expert'.

JUDGE: Really, really, gentlemen. Is all this acrimony necessary?

HARRICAN (*still making the most of his red herring*): Your Lordship will note that I am in no way responsible for introducing an unpleasant note into this trial. But to attack a state witness in such a manner—to accuse a Government Official of Contempt of Court . . . !

JUDGE: Yes, yes, yes. It seems to me that both sides are at fault.

THIN: Melud, I can only say that I stand by my objection.

HARRICAN: If it is to be alleged that the report is in any way improper, Mr. Ua Caoilte is entitled to an opportunity of explaining it, before being censured in this manner. And I must insist on the withdrawal by my friend of the expression, 'so-called expert'.

JUDGE: I am sure that Mr. Thin withdraws his remark. Whatever may be the merits of his objection, his remark was thoughtless and unnecessary.

THIN: I am quite prepared to withdraw my remark if my friend will withdraw this scandalous report.

HARRICAN: Scandalous! Ttt-ttt-ttt!

JUDGE: Now Mr. Harrican, without wishing to condone Mr. Thin's violence, you must admit that your expert's report does require some explanation.

HARRICAN: Which I am quite sure he is ready to offer, melud, if given an opportunity. However, lest it might seem that the witness is in any way biased in the matter I am agreeable to the expression 'murdered' being deleted from the report, provided it is understood that I am only doing so for the sake of peace.

JUDGE: Very reasonable of you, Mr. Harrican. Now Mr. Thin, what have you to say to that?

THIN: Melud, nobody can concede an untenable position more gracefully than my learned friend. But he cannot manœuvre me out of my right to cross-examine this witness.

HARRICAN: My dear fellow, he's yours. Cross-examine away. You may have him at once.

THIN: Well, Mr. Ua Caoilte, I suppose you recognize the fact that you have overstepped the mark?

UA CAOILTE (*furious*) : I do not, sir.

THIN: Really. Your head is bloody but unbowed, eh?

UA CAOILTE: My head is not even bloody, sir. Anything I said I am prepared to stand over.

THIN: Well, well. Even this word that your counsel has been wise enough to abandon.

UA CAOILTE: I am in the hands of the Court as to what shall be struck out of my report.

THIN: But you don't change your opinion?

UA CAOILTE: I do not, sir. I am not an amateur. I am a responsible official with expert qualifications, which I am prepared to state any time you like. You seem to wish to cast doubts upon my qualifications but . . .

JUDGE: Now Mr. Ua Caoilte, I am quite sure that nobody wishes to cast any doubts whatever upon your qualifications.

UA CAOILTE: My Lord, with respect, this gentleman wishes to do so. I don't deny that my report may err in its legal phraseology and I bow to the Court's ruling on that point. But in its statement of scientific fact I am prepared to stand over every word of it.

THIN: Don't be absurd, my good man. Is it a matter of scientific fact that Dr. Chavasse murdered his wife? By what process of observation can you reach that conclusion?

UA CAOILTE: Pardon me while I read it. (*He reads the report*) I do not say that Dr. Chavasse murdered his wife. I simply state that she was murdered, which is quite a different thing.

THIN: It's exactly the same thing. Don't quibble.

UA CAOILTE: I don't agree that it's the same thing. The one might be a matter of scientific deduction while the other is a matter of inference, which is quite outside my province as a pathologist.

THIN: So you would have us believe that there are ways by which you as a pathologist can deduce as a matter of scientific fact that Mrs. Chavasse was murdered?

UA CAOILTE: Yes, I should say there were.

THIN: How can you tell such a thing?

UA CAOILTE: Oh, there are various ways.

THIN: Tell me one of them.

UA CAOILTE: Well . . . the condition of the body for instance.

THIN: The condition of the body? And what does that mean, may I ask?

UA CAOILTE: These are scientific matters. They are difficult to explain to a layman.

THIN: And that is your evidence?

UA CAOILTE: In this case, yes.

THIN: The verdict of infallible science. You claim infallibility, I presume?

UA CAOILTE: I claim the right to believe the evidence of my own eyes, sir.

THIN: From the condition of the body. A matter too difficult to explain to us laymen.

UA CAOILTE: Well, in this case . . .

THIN: But sufficiently convincing in your own estimation to send a man to the gallows.

UA CAOILTE: I resent that. I have no wish to send anybody to the gallows. I don't like your manner.

THIN: Thank you, Mr. Ua Caoilte. That is all.

UA CAOILTE: But I insist on explaining . . .

THIN: That is all, Mr. Ua Caoilte. I have finished.

HARRICAN: Let him answer.

UA CAOILTE: I haven't finished. I want to explain the position.

THIN: I am sure the jury understand the position perfectly and will draw its own conclusions.

UA CAOILTE: But I have been asked a question, My Lord. Am I not going to be given an opportunity of answering it?

JUDGE: What's that? What is the question?

HARRICAN: It's all right, Mr. Ua Caoilte. His Lordship will allow you to explain yourself in re-examination.

JUDGE: Yes, Mr. Harrican. I would rather like to have all this cleared up. Proceed.

HARRICAN (feeling his way): Arising out of my friend's cross-examination, I take it that there are different ways in which Tincture of Sinacide could be administered?

UA CAOILTE: Naturally.

HARRICAN: It might, for instance, be administered in small doses over a long period. Or it might be taken in one large dose on a single occasion?

UA CAIOLTE: Quite so.

THIN: Don't lead the witness, please.

HARRICAN: You'll have very little to complain of if my leading question are all on matters as obvious as that. Tell me this: could Sinacide be administered in a single dose enough to cause death, without the victim being aware of it?

UA CAOILTE: No. I am sure it could not.

HARRICAN (*disappointed*): Oh. So you think that the victim would be aware of it?

UA CAOILTE: Probably.

THIN: He's mending his hand. He was quite definite the first time.

HARRICAN: Oh, very well. I yield the point to my friend. We're agreed then, that Mrs. Chavasse would hardly have died from a large single dose without protest?

THIN: Unless it was suicide.

HARRICAN: My friend is suggesting that if Mrs. Chavasse died from a single dose without protest it was probably suicide. What do you say to that?

UA CAOILTE: Assuming that there was somebody there to hear whether she protested or not.

THIN: Which there was in this case.

HARRICAN: Yes. We must admit that too. Mapother was apparently within earshot when she died, and both Mary Quirke and the child saw her shortly beforehand. (*He brightens perceptibly*) Now in the light of that, is there any way in which you can reconcile the possibility of her being murdered with the fact of her dying without protest?

UA CAOILTE (*brightening too*): Certainly there is.

HARRICAN: Will you explain, please.

UA CAOILTE: We can distinguish between two forms of Sinacidic poisoning—the acute and the chronic. The acute is the form you have just mentioned. If, however, Mrs. Chavasse died from chronic poisoning—that is to say, from small doses administered over a long period, she might easily have died without realizing what was the matter with her.

HARRICAN: Ah, now we're getting somewhere at last. Now tell me this, Mr. Ua Caoilte, supposing Mrs. Chavasse decided to commit suicide by taking Tincture of Sinacide, which would she be more likely to do? Would she take it in one dose or would she slowly poison herself over a long period?

THIN: I object to that question, melud.

JUDGE: It seems to me to be quite a legitimate question. What do you think, Mr. Ua Caoilte?

UA CAOILTE: My Lord, the answer is obvious. It is inconceivable that she would take a series of small doses.

HARRICAN: Now will you kindly explain more fully what you meant when you said that you could deduce from the condition of the body that she had been murdered.

UA CAOILTE: I meant that I was satisfied that Mrs. Chavasse died from chronic poisoning and not from acute. From which I consider I am justified in deducing that she did not commit suicide.

HARRICAN (*triumphantly*): Thank you, Mr. Ua Caoilte. That is all.

THIN: Wait one moment, please.

HARRICAN: I beg your pardon, Mr. Thin. You have already cross-examined this witness.

JUDGE: Yes, Mr. Thin. I think that I have given you very considerable latitude.

THIN: If your Lordship pleases.

(*He resumes his seat sulkily*)

HARRICAN: Now Mary Quirke.

REGISTRAR: Mary Quirke.

(*As she appears in the witness box there is an uneasy stirring in the court*)

REGISTRAR: Remove your glove, please. Raise the book in your right hand and repeat after me. (*She is duly sworn*) What's your name?

MARY (*very hangdog, in a low voice*): Mary Quirke.

HARRICAN: Speak up now, so that His Lordship and the jury can hear you. How long were you in Dr. Chavasse's employment?

MARY: Four years and three months, sir.

HARRICAN: And how long before Mrs. Chavasse's death did she appear to be ailing?

MARY: About eighteen months, sir. Ever since the time that the Doctor . . .

THIN: I object.

JUDGE: What's that, Mr. Thin?

THIN: Melud, this is the lady who tenders the evidence to which I take exception. I rely on my learned friend not to ask her any question bearing on the portion of her deposition marked 'A,' until its admissibility has been ruled upon by Your Lordship.

JUDGE: Oh yes, of course. The portion marked 'A'.

THIN: Will Your Lordship hear me on this question now or does my learned friend prefer to finish with the rest of her evidence first?

HARRICAN: I am in His Lordship's hands.

JUROR: Excuse me, My Lord, but the jury are not quite clear about all this. We would like to see this portion marked 'A'.

JUDGE: Oh dear me, no. You shall see nothing of the sort until I have decided whether it is proper for you to have it.

JUROR: But sir, we find it confusing when everybody else seems to know what . . .

JUDGE: That will do, my man. Please don't interrupt. Now, Mr. Harrican, I think you had better proceed with the non-controversial portion of this witness's evidence. Then when that is disposed of we will consider the other matter.

HARRICAN: Very good, melud. Now, Quirke, tell me this. Did you ever hear Mrs. Chavasse complain about her health during her illness?

MARY: She complained that the Doctor . . .

THIN: Objection.

HARRICAN: Now Quirke, I must warn you only to answer exactly the questions I put to you.

MARY: Am I not to be allowed to say all I have to say?

JUDGE: No, my good woman. We are the judges of how much you are to say, and I hope you realize that you may be punished very severely if you attempt to misbehave.

WARY (*sulkily*): I only want to tell the truth.

JUDGE: Yes, my good woman, but everything you wish to say may not be evidence in the present case. Please remember that.

MARY: Yes, My Lord.

HARRICAN: You remember the day on which your mistress died?

MARY: Yes, sir.

HARRICAN: Were you in the house all the morning?

MARY: Yes, sir. Except for the time the Master sent me out with a message to fetch over Dr. Hollingshead.

HARRICAN: When was that?

MARY: About half past nine.

HARRICAN: And did you deliver the message?

MARY: Oh yes, sir. It wasn't my fault she wouldn't come. I told the Master I did my best to persuade her, sir, and he rang her up later and she came over then.

HARRICAN: Were you about the place when she arrived?

MARY: No, sir. But I came out to the hall soon after.

HARRICAN: Were you there when your Master told the Sergeant that your Mistress had died of gastro-enteritis?

MARY: I was indeed, sir. Dr. Hollingshead here will certify it, he said. And I saw her nod her head. So I said . . .

HARRICAN: That will do, Quirke. And now melud, I propose with your permission to examine this witness on the portion of her deposition marked 'A'. This evidence was tendered to the District Justice on the remand who admitted it subject to my friend's objection. I would strongly urge upon Your Lordship that an allegation such as this, and the corroborative letters we have already referred to are clearly admissible as showing the circumstances and position of the parties concerned in the alleged offence, on the authority of *Dowling* against *Dowling* ten Irish Common Law Reports at page two hundred and thirty-six.

JUDGE: Of course you oppose the admission of this evidence, Mr. Thin?

THIN: I most certainly do, melud. In my contention it has no possible connection with the present case. At best or at worst it is mere evidence of the accused's character, and has been introduced with the sole object of prejudicing the issue. Anything that occurred at all, took place almost two years before the death of Mrs. Chavasse.

HARRICAN: I don't know what my friend means by 'Prejudicing

the issue'. Is he suggesting that Miss Quirke is attempting to give false testimony? That her statement is perjured?

THIN: Not at all. Nothing could be further from my mind. So far as I am aware Miss Quirke is a most respectable woman and I suggest nothing of the kind against her.

JUDGE: Indeed I am quite sure she is, Mr. Thin, and I fail, to see any reason why she should attempt to influence this case improperly.

THIN: Nor do I, melud. I have nothing against Miss Quirke at all. I have no doubt whatever that she believes implicitly in everything she says in her deposition. I do not even deny its accuracy. All I say is that it is irrelevant, and that it is my learned friend who now seeks to introduce it without legal justification.

HARRICAN (*disappointed*): Ah!

JUDGE: Well, Mr. Harrican, what do you say to that? It seems to me that there is one serious gap in your case as presented so far, and evidence of this kind might repair it.

HARRICAN: I understand what Your Lordship means. It bears upon the question of motive.

JUDGE: Exactly. And that is why you are pressing the matter. Well, I will tell you what is in my mind. If you will tell me that you are in a position to call some further evidence to connect this—er—event, with the present charge I might hear you further on its admissibility. In other words, do you propose to offer it to the jury as an isolated incident occurring eighteen months before the supposed crime, or are you in a position to show it as part of a series of events culminating in the death of Mrs. Chavasse?

HARRICAN (*after some consultation with* POER): I had anticipated that question, melud, and I shall be quite frank when I say that I have no further evidence to show the *res gestae* during the intervening period. I simply tender the evidence for what it is worth and will bow to Your Lordship's ruling in the matter.

JUDGE: In that case I cannot see my way to admit either the evidence contained in the portion marked 'A', or the letters produced by the Sergeant. There is nothing that I can see to connect them directly with the present charge, except as mere

evidence of character which, as the case at present stands, the
State is not entitled to call.

HARRICAN (*shrugging his shoulders*): Then I have nothing further
to ask this witness, melud.

JUDGE: And you, Mr. Thin?

THIN: I do not propose to cross-examine her at all, melud.

HARRICAN: Then that concludes the case for the prosecution. You
may stand down, my good woman.

MARY: Stand down? But am I not to be allowed to . . .

JUDGE: Kindly be silent. You are not entitled to address the Court.
Go away when you are told.

(MARY *leaves the box, muttering*)

JUROR: Excuse me, My Lord.

JUDGE: Yes? Eh? What's that?

JUROR: Do I understand that the jury are not going to be allowed
to read these letters?

JUDGE: No, sir. They do not concern you, gentlemen. Your minds
must not be confused with irrelevancies.

JUROR: But we are confused, My Lord, and everybody else seems
to know what it's all about.

JUDGE: Oh, tut-tut. This will never do. Come, Mr. Thin, we are
waiting for you.

THIN (*with an air of confidence and satisfaction*): May it please
Your Lordship, Gentlemen of the Jury, you have now heard the
case which my learned friend has made out on behalf of the
State against Dr. Chavasse, and I have no hesitation in saying
that in the course of twenty years' experience at the Bar I have
never heard so flimsy and improbable a charge. Not all the well-
known eloquence and ingenuity of Mr. Harrican, not all the
intensive labours and researches of the guards nor the host of
witnesses, both expert and inexpert, that they have marshalled
together has been able to clothe this fantastic indictment with
even a threadbare cloak of credibility. What, gentlemen, are
they asking you to believe? That Dr. Chavasse, a highly qualified medical practitioner, has been guilty of the monstrous and
unnatural crime of slowly and in cold blood doing his wife to
death in the foulest and meanest of manners by small daily

doses of a deadly poison. And upon what evidence is this fantastic allegation based? Upon a few ambiguous words overheard by an uneducated and very long-winded cow-keeper, supported by a hysterical domestic servant. Upon a foolish but understandable attempt by the Doctor to cover up the shame of a family suicide. And upon the opinion of a young Assistant Pathologist who inspected the body several days after the death and has given his evidence here with a dogmatic, nay, pathetic belief in the infallibility of Science and of his own powers of observation, which you, gentlemen, will know how to treat without any prompting from me. It is sufficient for me to say that were the evidence twenty times as strong against him, there would still be one fatal—one unbridgable gap in my friend's case against the Doctor. I refer to the absence of any motive for so atrocious a crime. Gentlemen, need I do more than ask you, why in Heaven's name should Dr. Chavasse have murdered his wife? There is not one tittle of evidence, to answer that vital question. Gentlemen, if Dr. Chavasse is a wife-murderer, then any of us who have ever suffered a like bereavement might as well be saddled with a similar charge. If Dr. Chavasse can be convicted upon such trumpery nonsense as the evidence that has been submitted to you—an outcome of this trial that I do not contemplate for one moment—then, gentlemen, how many of us are secure from the threat of the hangman. And now, with Your Lordship's permission, before calling the accused himself I propose to take the evidence of my own expert witness, Dr. Anice Hollingshead.

REGISTRAR: Dr. Anice Hollingshead.

(ANICE *comes to the box and is sworn*)

THIN: Dr. Hollingshead, I believe that you are the Dispensary Doctor for the district.

ANICE: Yes.

THIN: You remember attending Mrs. Chavasse on the morning of her death?

ANICE: Yes.

THIN: Will you tell the Court in what condition you found her.

ANICE: She was lying unconscious in the sitting-room. From her appearance and from what Dr. Chavasse told me I was able to diagnose poisoning at once.

THIN: You have heard that a quantity of Sinacidic acid was found in the stomach afterwards?

ANICE: I have heard so. And having seen her *in extremis* I have no doubt whatever as to the cause of her death.

THIN: What did you do for her?

ANICE: Well, first I ascertained from Dr. Chavasse what had already been done. I understand that he gave her an emetic which she spat out, and also an adrenalin injection in the heart. We then gave her another injection, but it was no good. She was sinking rapidly and died in about ten minutes.

THIN: Now, Dr. Hollingshead, from your observation of the case, can you form any opinion as to whether the poisoning was chronic or acute?

ANICE: Well, of course, I had no opportunity of conducting a post mortem, but I would certainly say from what I saw of her that it was acute.

THIN: Thank you, Doctor. And now one other matter. Did you hear Dr. Chavasse say anything to the police about gastro-enteritis?

ANICE: No. I was in the next room when the Sergeant arrived. As far as I can recollect all that took place when I was present was that Carey said, 'You'll certify the death in the usual way', and Dr. Chavasse replied yes, that I would do so. I heard no mention of gastro-enteritis then.

THIN: Actually you never gave any certificate?

ANICE: Oh no. There was a post-mortem.

THIN: Thank you, Doctor. That is all.

(*He sits down, and* HARRICAN *rises*)

HARRICAN: What time was it when you went over, Doctor?

ANICE: Between eleven and twelve, I should think.

HARRICAN: So that you allowed over two hours to elapse before you condescended to attend this unfortunate woman?

ANICE: Oh no. I did not.

HARRICAN: You didn't? But you were sent for at half past nine.

ANICE: No. It was after eleven.

HARRICAN: Didn't you hear the evidence of Mary Quirke?

ANICE: Yes.

HARRICAN: You heard her say that she brought you a message from Doctor Chavasse at 9.30?

ANICE (*confused*): Yes—but—yes, I heard that.

HARRICAN: Are you suggesting that Mary Quirke is lying when she says she brought you that message at 9.30?

ANICE: Lying? No, I don't wish to suggest that.

HARRICAN: Then you admit you got the message?

ANICE: I suppose I must.

HARRICAN: Yet you didn't go over to attend to the woman until between eleven and twelve?

ANICE: No.

HARRICAN: Why not?

ANICE: I—I wasn't able to.

HARRICAN: Come now. Is Mary Quirke perjuring herself when she says that at first you refused to go, and that Chavasse had to telephone for you about an hour later?

ANICE: I have nothing to say against Mary Quirke's evidence.

HARRICAN: Well, well.

JUDGE: Just one moment, please. Dr. Hollingshead, am I right in thinking that you are the local Dispensary Doctor?

ANICE: Yes, My Lord.

JUDGE: And do I understand you to admit that you received a call to attend Dr. Chavasse's dying wife and that you refused to go?

ANICE: No, I went over, My Lord.

JUDGE: Almost two hours later. After at first refusing to go?

ANICE: No—I—

HARRICAN: Come now, Doctor. Is Quirke telling the truth or is she not?

ANICE: Yes. She is.

JUDGE: Bless my soul! This is a surprising state of affairs. Is this the way you usually carry out your duties, Doctor?

ANICE: I went over as soon as I could, My Lord.

JUDGE: As soon as you could! You allowed this unfortunate woman to lie there in agony for two hours and then you answered the call ten minutes before she finally expired?

ANICE: Well—I—I don't know what to say.

JUDGE: I think that the less said the better. It seems to me that this is a state of affairs that ought to be brought to the notice of the Medical Council?

HARRICAN: Melud, it does appear to be an extraordinary admission on Dr. Hollingshead's part. But maybe after a little consideration she can supply us with an explanation. Eh, Doctor?

ANICE: No. I have nothing to add.

HARRICAN: You got the message and you just wouldn't go. You were busy, perhaps?

ANICE: I suppose that was it.

JUDGE: Really, this is very, very shocking. I am amazed. In fact I am very much upset. Whatever may be the outcome of this case there are certain aspects which reflect no credit on any of the parties concerned. I can only hope that they have not escaped the attention of the press. Proceed, Mr. Harrican.

HARRICAN: Well, if that is really all Dr. Hollingshead has to tell us, I have nothing more to ask her.

(*He shrugs his shoulders and sits down*)

THIN: You can leave the box, Doctor. Call the prisoner, Frank Chavasse.

(CHAVASSE *takes* ANICE's *place and is sworn. He is in a state of some excitement*)

THIN: Dr. Chavasse, did you poison your wife?

CHAVASSE: I did not, sir.

THIN: Have you any idea as to how she received the poison that killed her?

CHAVASSE: I have no direct knowledge, but I am afraid that it was self-administered.

THIN: You mean, suicide?

CHAVASSE: I am afraid there is no doubt about it.

THIN: Have you any idea whether she could have had access to this poison herself?

CHAVASSE: Well, I had some Tincture of Sinacide in my poison cabinet.

THIN: Where is that?

CHAVASSE: In the dispensing room.

THIN: That is the room marked 'H' in the model of the house?

CHAVASSE: Yes.

THIN: It opens off the room where she died?

CHAVASSE: That is quite correct.

THIN: Could Mrs. Chavasse have got at it?

CHAVASSE: Yes, I suppose she could.

THIN: Did you keep it locked?

CHAVASSE: Yes, it was always locked—in theory at least. But she knew where she could get the key.

THIN: Then you didn't carry the key on your person?

CHAVASSE: I used to. Until my dispenser lost her key. Then I used to leave mine in a drawer where we could both get it. I had intended to have another key cut, but somehow it got put off from week to week.

THIN: Did your wife ever show any suicidal tendencies?

CHAVASSE: Not to my knowledge. But she had been ailing for some time before this.

THIN: What was the matter with her?

CHAVASSE: Oh neurosis, principally. She was an exceedingly nervous and difficult woman. Hysterical, I might almost say. She was approaching a troublesome time of life.

THIN: And now, Doctor, I am going to ask you a more serious question. It has been suggested here by Mapother, by Mary Quirke and by the guards themselves that you first attempted to put off the police with a story that your wife had died of gastro-enteritis . . . in fact, that you called in Dr. Hollingshead for the purpose of obtaining a false death certificate. Have you anything to say to that?

CHAVASSE: I can't understand Mapother's attitude towards me, but Mary Quirke is easily explained. She . . .

THIN: Never mind about her. What I asked you was whether you tried to conceal the real cause of death?

CHAVASSE: Yes, I must admit that at first I did hope to hush it up. It was foolish of me, I know. But after all, the scandal of a suicide . . . She couldn't have been responsible for what she did.

THIN: And that is the reason for your first statement to Sergeant Carey?

CHAVASSE: Yes, simply that. You see, suicide invariably raises questions of sanity.

THIN: And you have a child?

CHAVASSE: Yes, that's right. But I do most emphatically deny that there was ever any question of a false death certificate. I called in Dr. Hollingshead because I needed further medical assistance. That is all.

THIN: Thank you, Doctor.

(*He sits down*).

CHAVASSE: Thank you, Mr. Thin. But before I stand down I wish to explain about Mary Quirke.

THIN: No, Doctor. That is all, if you please.

JUDGE: Yes, Mr. Harrican?

HARRICAN: Your suggestion, Dr. Chavasse, is that your wife poisoned herself?

CHAVASSE: There is no question about it.

HARRICAN: And can you give us any reason for her committing so unaccountable an act?

CHAVASSE: Is it any more unaccountable than that I should have murdered her, as you suggest?

HARRICAN: Don't bother to ask me questions, Doctor. Is is I who have that privilege.

CHAVASSE: It was only a rhetorical question.

HARRICAN: Well, rhetoric apart, tell us something more about this poison cabinet of yours, Doctor. How much Sinacide was there in it?

CHAVASSE: Not very much. About ten grains in solution, I should think. Quite enough to cause death.

HARRICAN: And what was it kept in?

CHAVASSE: It was in a four-ounce bottle.

HARRICAN: Labelled?

CHAVASSE: Naturally. All my bottles are labelled.

HARRICAN: Labelled 'Poison'?

CHAVASSE: 'Poison'—I don't think so. It wasn't medicine. It was labelled 'Tinc. Sina.'—the pharmaceutical abbreviation.

HARRICAN: Doesn't the Act provide that all such bottles must be labelled 'Poison'?

CHAVASSE: Not surely in the privacy of one's own surgery?

HARRICAN: I see. You medical men take a free and easy view of Acts of Parliament. Can you let us see this bottle?

CHAVASSE: No, I don't think so.

HARRICAN: Why not?

CHAVASSE: I don't know. I looked for it, but it seems to have been mislaid.

HARRICAN: Really? Mislaid! Rather surprising that?

CHAVASSE: Maybe. But I can't see how it matters.

HARRICAN: Your suggestion then, is that not only did your wife poison herself, but having done so, she then proceeded to hide or destroy the bottle?

CHAVASSE: I'm not suggesting anything. All I know is, that like many other things in my house, it has disappeared.

HARRICAN: What do you mean by that?

CHAVASSE: I mean that with Mary Quirke in my house I am never surprised at anything disappearing.

HARRICAN: You're not suggesting that she has taken this bottle for some reason or other?

CHAVASSE: I am not suggesting anything. I am stating that this woman, who is at the back of these whole proceedings, is a thief and a liar.

THIN: Control yourself, Doctor.

CHAVASSE: Why should I control myself? I have been accused of murder by that woman and it is only right that the jury should know the reason why.

JUDGE: Now, Dr. Chavasse, I don't know what has passed between you and your counsel, but I am sure that you would be well advised to leave the conduct of your case to him, and confine yourself strictly to what you are asked.

CHAVASSE: My lord, I have answered my counsel's questions as fully and as truthfully as I can, but I am now in the hands of Mr. Harrican and I claim the right to answer him no less fully.

JUDGE: Quite so. Quite so. I am sure no one wishes to prompt you.

Your evidence is your own concern. And . . . ahem . . . I may add, your own risk.

THIN: Melud, I don't think that Dr. Chavasse fully realizes the position . . .

CHAVASSE (*venomously*): I realize that there is a general conspiracy on the part of everybody to whitewash Mary Quirke, and that I am expected to sit quietly in the dock and hear her described as an honest and respectable woman and patted on the back even by my own counsel, when all kinds of lying suggestions are being made and even admitted against me and Dr. Hollingshead.

JUDGE: I see.

CHAVASSE: My Lord, I have been told by my own advisers not to tell the truth about that woman for reasons of policy. But there are limits to the amount of trickery I can put up with when it's she and not I who ought to be on trial.

HARRICAN: That is a very serious allegation to make, Dr. Chavasse.

CHAVASSE: That is what it's intended to be. I don't see why the jury shouldn't know that it was she who first trumped up this charge against me to save herself from jail. It was I who sent for the police on the day of my wife's death and it was in order to arrest Mary Quirke.

HARRICAN: Really?

CHAVASSE (*hysterically*): The woman is a thief—a petty pilferer. Ever since my wife's illness she has been robbing us. And as for her story about taking my message to Dr. Hollingshead, it's a lie from start to finish. The jury will note that this is the kind of person—'this respectable woman' as she has been called—on whose evidence I am being accused!

(*There is a pause*)

JUDGE: Well, Mr. Thin. This puts a new complexion on the case.

THIN (*hopelessly*): Melud, the matter has passed out of my hands.

HARRICAN (*with a new manner*): This—er—new development, melud, will of course be conveyed to the Attorney General, and I have no doubt that if Dr. Chavasse will swear the necessary information a warrant will be issued at once for Quirke's arrest.

JUDGE: Quite so. If that is what Dr. Chavasse wishes.

CHAVASSE: It is certainly what I wish.

HARRICAN: It shall be done. And now, melud, to return to the present case. Under Section 1(*f*) of the Criminal Justice (Evidence) Act 1924, I am of course precluded from asking Dr. Chavasse any question tending to show that he has committed any offence other than the one with which he is charged. This protection however no longer applies if the conduct of the defence is of such a nature as to make imputations against the character of any of the State's witnesses. Dr. Chavasse has now made the gravest of charges against the character of one of my witnesses, and I am therefore entitled in reply to cross-examine him upon his own character, after which, subject to Your Lordship's permission, I propose to recall Mary Quirke for the purpose of examining her upon the portion of her deposition marked 'A'.

JUDGE: Well, Mr. Thin? There appears to be no answer to that?

THIN: I am in Your Lordship's hands.

JUDGE: Your application is granted, Mr. Harrican. Proceed with your cross-examination. After which you may recall the witness Quirke.

HARRICAN: Dr. Chavasse, is it true that prior to your wife's death you had been living in adultery with Dr. Anice Hollingshead, and that eighteen months ago you both procured an abortion?

Curtain

ACT THREE

ACT THREE

SCENE 1

Six months later. The State Solicitor's office.
(POER *is at his desk. The telephone rings*)

POER (*into the telephone*): Yes. No, I will not see Mapother again. I explained to him what the position was three weeks ago, at the time of the appeal. What does he want this time? No, I have nothing further to say. I warned him at the time we didn't want him. Tell him—what's that? Oh, all right, I'll see him this once. Who did you say was in the small office? Miss Hollings-head. Is that Anice Hollingshead? Did she say what she wants? Well, better send her in first and tell Mapother to wait.

(*He hangs up the receiver. Presently* ANICE *enters*)

ANICE: Mr. Poer, I insist upon seeing you.

POER: Won't you sit down? This is an unexpected pleasure.

ANICE: I assure you, it is no pleasure to me.

POER: Then perhaps the sooner we get our interview over the better. I am not responsible for it.

ANICE: I wish I knew just how much you are responsible for. I wish I knew who was really at the back of all that has happened to Dr. Chavasse and me.

POER: You have something to say besides that, I presume?

ANICE: Mr. Poer, I can't stand this suspense any longer. Why don't you arrest me too, and have done with it?

POER: You feel that you deserve to be arrested?

ANICE: It isn't a question of deserts. After what has been done to Frank Chavasse I can expect anything from you.

POER: I'm not aware of doing anything to Dr. Chavasse. If you want my opinion, he got a remarkably fair trial.

ANICE: Fair! With such an outcome!

POER: Perfectly fair. And what about the outcome? He wanted to

147

jail Mary Quirke. My object was to jail him. Very well. Now we're both satified, so why complain?

ANICE: He wasn't given a chance.

POER: On the contrary. Thin had us beaten to the ropes. A very clever piece of work it was, too. However, we can still rely upon the good old maxim of 'Set a thief to catch a thief.'

ANICE: He didn't understand the position. If he had known . . .

POER: But I hear that he *was* advised to leave Quirke out of it.

ANICE: He should have been told why.

POER: My dear Doctor, when you prescribe a diet for a patient, do you feel called upon to explain the mechanics of the stomach as well? If you pay for professional advice you should take it, and not set up a howl if things go wrong when you don't. Chavasse simply preferred to give way to the luxury of losing his temper, and that's the long and the short of it.

ANICE: I don't care what you say or how you put it. No trial that ends in the conviction of an innocent man is a fair trial.

POER: Even when he has nobody to blame but himself?

ANICE: Why, that only makes it all the worse. Can't you see that? It doesn't seem to be a matter of truth or falsity, of justice or injustice to you lawyers. It's all a sort of a game, that you win or lose according to the rules. Frank hasn't been convicted because he was guilty, but simply because he couldn't play the game as well as you. You admit it yourself.

POER: You realize that the death sentence has been commuted?

ANICE: Do you claim credit for that? How like a lawyer! You condemn an innocent man to death and then propose to be thanked for keeping him in jail for the rest of his life instead!

POER: I am not asking to be thanked. The reprieve was none of my doing.

ANICE: Better to hang him than to give him a living death!

POER: Miss Hollingshead, I will tell you frankly that in my private opinion any man who did what Dr. Chavasse has been convicted of doing ought to be hanged.

ANICE: And an innocent man ought to go free.

POER: Yes. I agree with you there. Either he did it or he didn't do it. He should either die or go free. Mercy is no solution.

ANICE: He doesn't want mercy. He wants justice.

POER: Which I believe he got.

ANICE: Then why was the death sentence commuted?

POER: It is often the way. I don't profess to be in the confidence of the Executive Council.

ANICE: You know quite well why it was. It was because they had a doubt. And if they have any doubt, isn't he entitled to the benefit of it?

POER: Miss Hollingshead, I take it that you have not come to see me in order to have the death sentence reinstated?

ANICE: I have come to ask you what you intend to do about me. If Dr. Chavasse is guilty, do you not consider me guilty too?

POER: I'm afraid I'm not at liberty to divulge . . .

ANICE: Mr. Poer, for months you have been playing cat and mouse with me. At one moment I think I am going to be arrested, and then nothing happens. I tell you I can't stand it any longer. I appeal to you to put me out of this torment.

POER (*after a moment's pause*): I have no wish to torment you, Miss Hollingshead. If the matter lay in my hands, be assured you would soon be put out of doubt.

ANICE: I can't understand you. Are you unspeakably callous or just blindly stupid?

POER: Neither, I hope.

ANICE: Then, can't you see what it means to me? I would rather be tried and convicted than have this hanging over my head any longer. My life is ruined anyhow. You must realize what they are all saying about me. If you think the same, I deserve to be treated like Frank. If you don't amn't I entitled to be publicly acquitted?

POER: I do appreciate that, Miss Hollingshead, and there is a lot in what you say. So although I can't pretend to offer much sympathy in the circumstances, I will tell you in confidence that unless something further turns up, it's unlikely that the Attorney General will move against you.

ANICE: But you suspect me?

POER: I won't deny that the matter has been considered. But suspicion is not legal proof, and in spite of what you think of them, the Law Officers do attempt to take a humane and common-sense view of their duties, especially where women are concerned. As a matter of fact you were rather expected to take the hint and disappear quietly.

ANICE: To run away, in fact.

POER: Well, in my profession I have long ago given up making prophecies about other people's conduct. If we were wrong, and you would prefer to be prosecuted . . .

ANICE (*sobbing*): Oh, God, is there no real humanity in the world? How I hate you and all that you stand for. Yes, I want to be prosecuted. I'd rather have it that way.

POER: Miss Hollingshead, you are either a very foolish woman or a very daring one.

ANICE: Perhaps I'm an honest one. That possibility doesn't seem to have occurred to you.

POER: Your hostility certainly makes it hard for me to believe otherwise. You know, Doctor, I'm not really a callous man or a particularly stupid one. The key to my attitude is very simple. I believe that Dr. Chavasse poisoned his wife. That's all.

ANICE: But why? Are you infallible? What right have you to sit in judgment on him?

POER: None whatever. But it's my lot to be engaged on a job where I find it difficult not to exercise my own intelligence. If that makes it hard for me to feel much sympathy for the guilty, I can only plead on the other hand that just as frequently it enables me to assist the innocent and the irresponsible.

ANICE: But what is it that makes you so sure about Frank?

POER: I can't see why I should discuss it with you, Miss Hollingshead, but I will. Apart from the positive evidence, all of which points clearly to a murder, there's nothing whatever to support the alternative possibility of suicide. People don't commit suicide without leaving some trace. But here there is nothing. Nothing to suggest that Mrs. Chavasse went to the cupboard and did herself to death. Not a bottle, nor a glass, not even a spoon. That means that something has been concealed, and concealment implies guilt.

ANICE: That's not conclusive—just because a bottle is lost.

POER: Destroyed, you mean. Bottles of Sinacide are not lost. Dr. Chavasse destroyed it and its contents because he originally intended to deny possessing the stuff at all. He forgot that we would trace it in the books of the local chemist.

ANICE: That is not so.

POER: Why should I believe you, Miss Hollingshead, while you both still persist in lying on vital matters?

ANICE: How am I lying?

POER: Well, you asked me, so I'll tell you. You are suggesting that Mrs. Chavasse committed suicide. Her only motive for doing so could have been her knowledge that her husband was having relations with you. And yet you would have us believe that you and Doctor Chavasse had not spoken to each other for eighteen months before her death. Isn't that rather inconsistent?

ANICE: She wouldn't believe it.

POER (*shaking his head*): No, Doctor. Suicide or murder, she knew quite well that you were associating.

ANICE (*after a pause*): If only I could see him once.

POER: I am sorry, but the law does not allow that so long as you are under suspicion.

ANICE: Is it true that he tried to kill himself?

POER: He threatened to. . . . Prison psychosis. That happens often. We don't take such threats very seriously. But naturally we have taken necessary precautions. Don't let it worry you.

ANICE (*stares intently for a moment*): I must confess.

POER: I'm listening.

ANICE: Frank and I were intimate to the last . . .

POER: I'm listening.

ANICE: You want to know the truth?

POER: Only the truth.

ANICE: I killed Mrs. Chavasse.

POER: You killed Mrs. Chavasse? And why did you do that?

ANICE: I loved Chavasse. That woman destroyed him. She was petty and mean; she tormented him; she made his life miserable. I couldn't bear the way she nagged at him.

POER: Why didn't Dr. Chavasse divorce his wife?

ANICE: He wanted to at first. But then he hesitated. . . . He couldn't make up his mind; he seemed incapable of deciding one way or the other.

POER: And you wanted him to decide?

ANICE: Yes.

POER: He . . . After your confession, you understand I must arrest you.

ANICE: Will Frank be released?

POER: If it is proved that he really knew nothing about the murder —yes.

ANICE: He knew nothing.

POER: Then all the time you have been lying?

ANICE: Yes.

POER: You say you love Dr. Chavasse, yet you allowed him, the man you love, to be condemned to death for a crime that you yourself committed? (ANICE *says nothing*) Why didn't you speak up before? Were you able to commit a second murder, to deliver to hangmen the man you pretend to love? Why did you not speak before? Tell me. (ANICE *says nothing*) Then I will tell you. We prosecuters are not as slipshod as you think. We cruel servants of the law sometimes have the strange task of protecting certain people from the law and even from themselves. This attempt to sacrifice yourself to save Dr. Chavasse is naive—and allow me to say it . . . a trifle cheap.

ANICE: And how may one call your successful attempt to inform the jury about our intimacy? Because you knew that they would be convinced that a married doctor who was able to have an affair with a woman and even arrange an abortion for her— would be just the man to murder his wife. You moved heaven and earth to put it before the jury.

POER: You have to blame Dr. Chavasse. If he had not attacked my witness Mary Quirke . . . I would not . . .

ANICE: Please, please . . . ! You call that justice! I do not envy you Mr. Poer. You have given me a lesson which I shall never forget. You taught me to see.

POER: And what are you seeing?

ANICE: I learned that the lie of our trial was only one of many lies which our world is built.

POER: My dear Dr. Hollingshead, I have had much experience in my life, believe me, but what I have learned is that lie and truth are oft so mingled that only God may know to disentangle them. You are really mistaken, Dr. Hollingshead, if you think it is my job to keep an innocent man in prison. But you must recognize that you have been unable to produce any proof of his innocence. On the other hand there is an almost infallible test that I always apply in these situations—and that is the attitude of the independent witnesses. Why would they be so hostile if they did not actually know something?

ANICE: But surely that woman Quirke . . .

POER: Never mind Quirke. She doesn't count. But what about Mapother? Could the Doctor have had a more faithful friend and advocate up to the time of the death?

ANICE: Mapother! I can't understand about him. We never did him any harm. Quite the reverse.

POER: Suppose it was because he knew your story was a lie—that you and Dr. Chavasse had not broken off your relationship in spite of what you swore to the contrary?

ANICE: No, no! It can't be that!

POER: Would you like to ask him? He's outside now in one of the waiting-rooms.

ANICE: Here! Now! Yes, let me speak to him.

POER: Very well. You prefer to be alone?

ANICE: No. I'm not afraid of anything he can say. I'll talk to him in front of you.

POER: It may do you no good, Miss Hollingshead.

ANICE: I prefer it that way.

POER: As you wish. (*He picks up the telephone*) Send in Mapother. (*They sit in silence until* MAPOTHER *enters*)

MAPOTHER: Ah, may the merciful God be praised: Is that you, my dear sir, at long last? I've been waiting to see you many's the day about this little matter of my expenses general and particular. Mr. Poer, my dear sir, I would be the last to trouble you over so paltry a matter but . . .

POER: We'll discuss your expenses later, Mapother. Here is Miss

Hollingshead who wishes to speak to you. (MAPOTHER *looks at her in suspicious silence*)

ANICE: Good afternoon, Dominick.

MAPOTHER: It is and it isn't, my good lady. There's many a bad afternoon that is made the better by a thoughtful act towards the poor and lowly and there's many a fine afternoon that is darkened by a false friend.

ANICE: Dominick, we were good friends once, weren't we?

MAPOTHER: I'll not deny it, ma'am, for to deny it would soil your gracious presence with a lie.

ANICE: And you were a good friend to Dr. Chavasse, too?

MAPOTHER: I was indeed. Ah, God forgive me if I should ever harbour a dark thought against a fellow sufferer in this Vale of Tears.

ANICE: Then, Dominick, why did you give evidence against him? . . . your friend who had done so much for you?

MAPOTHER: My dear madam, neither man, woman, child nor priest shall ever say that Dominick is not a true friend to his friends. If anyone had told me a year ago that Dominick Mapother would ever raise his voice against the Doctor, I'd have felled him with a mighty blow. But I'm telling you no lie when I say that it was the Doctor himself who turned out to be no friend of Dominick's.

ANICE: But Dominick, he was. I know he was.

MAPOTHER: Fair words, fair words, my dear lady. That's all. Oh, it grieves me more than it grieves you. Shall I tell you the story of my cow?

POER: No.

ANICE: How can you speak of him like that, Dominick, when you remember all that he did for you and your cow?

MAPOTHER: Little enough, ma'am, when it came to the great crisis. She asked for bread and he gave her a stone. And she, poor beast, R.I.P., *in articulo mortis*.

ANICE: Didn't he give you medicine for her?

MAPOTHER: Medicine, my dear ma'am! A stingy couple of spoonfuls in an old black bottle. Is it any wonder that on administering the same the noble beast broke into shudderings and perspiration, and passed from this heartless sphere of mortal indifference in the short space of half an hour?

POER: A black bottle? And Dr. Chavasse gave to you?

MAPOTHER: Yes, my dear sir. At least, if I remember rightly, he told the child to give it to me.

POER: What was the child doing with it?

MAPOTHER: Playing with it, I recollect, in the garden.

POER: Have you still got it?

MAPOTHER: Indeed, my dear sir, I remarked upon it myself a day or two ago, standing on a shelf in the byre, a monument to the selfishness and indifference of mankind.

POER (*rising*): Mapother, I would like to see that bottle.

CURTAIN

SCENE 2

The same. Two days later.

(POER *is at his desk. Before him is a small cardboard box.* UA CAOILTE *enters*)

POER: Come in, Mr. Ua Caoilte. I'm sorry for having kept you waiting.

UA CAOILTE: Conus ata tu.

POER: The same to you. Won't you sit down?

UA CAOILTE: Go raibh maith agat. Abair do ghno ma se do thoil e.

POER: I presume you speak English, Mr. Ua Caoilte?

UA CAOILTE (*with a superior smile*): Certainly, Mr. Poer, if necessary. I would have thought, however, that between two Government officials . . . Still, if you have not the Irish . . . (*He shrugs*)

POER: When next we're having a discussion on politics or literature I shall be delighted to talk to you in a wide variety of languages. But at present I wish to speak to you as a practical pathologist, and if you don't mind I think we'd better stick to English.

UA CAOILTE: A pity, Mr. Poer. Particularly in your position. Amongst our qualifications . . .

POER: Amongst your qualifications as a pathologist is a sound knowledge of Gaelic and an uncle in the Passport Office. I know that, Mr. Ua Caoilte.

UA CAOILTE (*rising*): I am afraid I don't like your tone. Are you trying to be offensive? Because if so . . .

POER: No, I'm not. Sit down. I'm sorry for losing my temper, but I must ask you to be serious.

UA CAOILTE: I don't know what authority you have to call me over here from my laboratory. I'm an exceedingly busy man and I'm not aware that I am under your jurisdiction.

POER: I don't claim any authority over you whatsoever, Mr. Ua Caoilte. But I have something of very great importance that I want to discuss with you. A cigarette?

UA CAOILTE: Well then, please state your business at once and allow me to get back to my work.

POER: It's about the Chavasse case. You remember it?

UA CAOILTE (*immediately on his guard*): Oh! That! Yes. Well, what about it?

POER: I think I may say that it was largely on your expert evidence that Chavasse was found guilty.

UA CAOILTE: A most unsavoury case. The man's own character was quite enough to convict him.

POER: His character was probably at the back of the verdict. But your evidence was the occasion, Mr. Ua Caoilte. The rest was largely suspicion.

UA CAOILTE: Well, have you any complaints? It's your business to get convictions, I presume.

POER: It's not my business to get convictions. It is my business to see that every relevant fact is laid before the Court, whether for or against the prisoner.

UA CAOILTE: And how, may I ask, does all this concern me?

POER: Mr. Ua Caoilte, when you had examined the body and found Sinacide, you sent us in a report to the effect that this woman had been murdered.

UA CAOILTE (*after a moment's hesitation*): Yes. There was more than enough poison in the remains to cause death.

POER: I used the word 'murdered'.

UA CAOILTE (*blustering*): Yes, I know, I know. I've been asked about that before and I have explained fully. Sinacidical poisoning may either be chronic or acute and . . .

POER: Quite so. But at what stage of the case did that aspect of the matter occur to you?

UA CAOILTE: What do you mean?

POER: I mean, did you reason all that out for yourself when you examined the body, or did Harrican put it into your head when you were in the witness box?

UA CAOILTE: I resent that suggestion, Mr. Poer.

POER: I can't help that. I want to know.

UA CAOILTE (*rising*): If that is your attitude to me, sir, I don't see that any good can come from continuing this discussion. I have given my evidence, and that is all I have to say. Slan agat.

POER: One moment please, Mr. Ua Caoilte. This is not the time for either of us to stand on our dignity. A man has only just escaped the gallows with a life sentence thanks to you and me, and there is something we have got to clear up.

UA CAOILTE: I have nothing whatever to clear up.

POER: Well, I have if you haven't. You remember that we commented adversely on the fact that Dr. Chavasse couldn't or wouldn't produce his Sinacide bottle?

UA CAOILTE: I remember something of the sort.

POER: Well, I have now found that bottle. It was taken by mistake from Dr. Chavasse's house on the day of his wife's death. And here it is. (*Opens the cardboard box*)

UA CAOILTE: Well? What significance is there in that?

POER: Perhaps a lot. You may remember that amongst the other activities of our zealous policeman, he took the finger-prints of the corpse. Well, I have had this bottle examined, and in spite of the lapse of time we have found that it still bears discernable fingerprints. And amongst these fingerprints are some of those of the dead woman.

(*Pause*)

UA CAOILTE (*shaken*): I still don't see the significance.

POER: The significance! Why man, it proves that not only could she have poisoned herself but that she actually had the bottle in her hands before her death! It means that if you are wrong about the poisoning being chronic, or even uncertain about it, the trial must be set aside.

UA CAOILTE: Why should I be wrong?

POER: Why should anybody be wrong? Because you made a mistake, that's why.

UA CAOILTE: Are you casting doubts upon my abilities as a pathologist, because if so . . .?

POER: Damn your abilities, sir. I'm asking you whether you mightn't have blundered?

UA CAOILTE: What do you know about it? I am a scientist and when I'm asked my opinion . . .

POER: By what tests did you determine the poisoning to be chronic?

UA CAOILTE: By various tests.

POER: Mention one.

UA CAOILTE: Well, by the distribution of the poison in the body.

POER: How can you ascertain that?

UA CAOILTE: By an examination of the various organs.

POER: What difference would you expect to find in these?

UA CAOILTE: All sorts of differences.

POER: For instance?

UA CAOILTE: Well, for instance, the hair . . .

POER: Did you examine the hair?

UA CAOILTE: The hair? What business is it of yours?

POER: Did you examine the hair?

UA CAOILTE: No, I didn't, but . . .

POER: I see. You would be able to tell by the hair and you didn't examine the hair.

UA CAOILTE: Why should I? The woman was rotten with the stuff. It was a clear case.

POER: Case of what?

UA CAOILTE: Of poisoning—(*he corrects himself*) Of murder. It's the same thing in this case.

POER: And that assumption was the basis of your evidence?

UA CAOILTE: Mr. Poer, I will not be browbeaten by you. I tell you I will not permit it.

POER: Come now. Do you still stand over your report?

UA CAOILTE: Believe me, you'll hear more of this. I'll carry the matter further. I'm not under your jurisdiction and you have no right to . . .

POER: On your evidence depends whether a man serves a life sentence or not. Have you considered that?

UA CAOILTE: You are trying to injure my professional reputation and . . .

POER: Yes, isn't that the crux of the whole matter? Your professional reputation. My God man, why should I want to injure you? Forget about your professional reputation for a moment and consider what depends on you. We all make mistakes. I'm in this myself just as deeply as you are. But we have got to face it—both of us.

UA CAOILTE: It wasn't my evidence that convicted him. He seemed to me to be a pretty shady character generally.

POER: Maybe he is. Maybe he ought to be in jail for something else. But we are now discussing whether he's a murderer. That's just the difficulty that you and I are faced with, Ua Caoilte. We come up against so many shady characters . . . every day we see so many rascals escaping their due deserts in the courts that we are apt to play too hard for our side, whenever we can. It's all a game, Ua Caoilte, as somebody said to me a day or two ago . . . a game where the rules are all on the side of the clever ones . . . the sly ones. We intend them to protect the innocent, but in nine cases out of ten their only use is to enable clever scoundrels to get off. And so we get cynical about them and forget that we still owe a duty to the fools . . . the fools there are no rules to protect. I'm not claiming any jurisdiction over you, Ua Caoilte. We're each servants of something far bigger than ourselves—Science and Justice. We're neither of us infallible . . . God help us. But that's no reason for throwing up the sponge. If we really believe in what we serve we can only do our best, and when something goes wrong with the works, try to right it as best we can, remembering that it isn't the fault of Science or Justice when these things happen. It is our fault . . . men's fault. Justice may be blind, but she's no harlot. If I didn't believe that and cling to it, how long do you suppose I'd be able to do my job? And what real service do you suppose you'll ever be able to do for Science if you are prepared to prostitute her to your professional reputation?

UA CAOILTE (*shaken*): I know you mean well, Poer, but . . .

POER: Of course. We both mean well. Perhaps even the man in jail meant well. And on that basis I will ask you my question again. Are you prepared to swear beyond all reasonable doubt that Mrs. Chavasse died from sinacidic poisoning, and that the poisoning was chronic and not acute? (*There is a pause. Then* UA CAOILTE *takes a deep breath and shouts furiously*)

UA CAOILTE: No, sir! I am not!

POER (*shouting back*): Thank you, Mr. Ua Caoilte. (*He picks up the telephone.*) Get me the Attorney General!

CURTAIN

SCENE 3

The hall of Dr. Chavasse's house, a few weeks later. The place has been shut up and the furniture is covered with dust sheets. (Presently a key is inserted in the hall door and ANICE comes in followed by MAPOTHER)

ANICE: Come on in, Dominick, if you really want to help.

MAPOTHER: I do indeed, my dear lady. Any little service that can render the home-coming a joyous one. Oh, a depressing spectacle! Allow me.

ANICE: It's very kind of you. I'd like to have the place in some sort of order for him.

MAPOTHER: A pleasure, madam.

ANICE: Isn't it wonderful, Dominick! I can hardly believe it's true. Did you see the crowd waiting at the station?

MAPOTHER: Did I see the crowd? My dear lady, am I not the fons and origo of the Reception Committee? Am I not the guiding genius of the popular movement to give the Doctor the rousing welcome home that he deserves? Have I not carried the struggle on to my own domestic hearth and had words with my sister's husband over the propriety of calling out the Town Band?

ANICE (*laughing*): Oh, Dominick, not that band?

MAPOTHER: Undoubtedly, my dear lady, were it not for the unconstitutional act of my said brother-in-law in locking himself up with the principal instruments. However, all may yet be well, for I left my enlightened supporters pressing their unanswerable arguments upon him through the keyhole.

ANICE: Now, Dominick, we mustn't have any trouble. Not to-day. Please.

MAPOTHER: Ah, my dear madam, in the name of fair play and civic virtue what harm is there in taking an odd slap or two at the Scribes and Pharisees?

ANICE: There's so much for us to be thankful for. We mustn't let anything spoil his homecoming.

MAPOTHER: That's right, ma'am. And who am I to cast the first stone? Can Humanity analyse the inscrutable ways of Providence? There was I, head and foremost of his persecutors, like Saul of Tarsus, also called Paul. And all out of consideration for my unfortunate cow. Little did I know how guiltless he was in that matter. A solemn thought.

ANICE: Well, it's all over now, Dominick. Besides think what you did for him in the end?

MAPOTHER: Yes, my dear lady, what a blessing it is to know that in spite of everything I was the poor humble tool called upon to produce the magic talisman that set the sufferer free.

ANICE: You may be sure he bears nobody any ill will.

MAPOTHER: Ill will, is it? Who could attribute such a sentiment to the man whose first kindly act was to promise your humble servant another cow? What generosity! What magnanimity!

ANICE: There. Now the hall looks a little better. I wonder have we time for the sitting-room? He must be due by now.

MAPOTHER: Yes indeed, ma'am. Could you tell me this now? What does it cost a man to insure a good cow? (*There is a knock at the door*)

ANICE (*laughing*): Oh, Dominick, I'm so happy! (*She opens the door.* POER *and* SERGEANT CAREY *are on the step*)

ANICE: Oh!

CAREY: Good afternoon, miss. I've come to leave in the Doctor's papers and letters.

ANICE: Thank you, Sergeant. Just put them there on the table.

POER: How do you do?

ANICE (*polite, but on her guard*): Good afternoon, Mr. Poer.

CAREY: We'll all be glad to see the Doctor back.

ANICE: I'm sure you will, Sergeant. Excuse me, please. (*She goes off into the sitting-room*)

POER: Quite a crowd outside. A civic welcome?

MAPOTHER: And doesn't he deserve it, my good man, after all he's been through?

POER: I'm glad the people are taking it that way.

CAREY: Well sir, I'll not deny that the town is a bit divided. There's a great body of pious folk that still looks on the moral side of it. The clergy are saying that even if not legally guilty he still has a moral responsibility for driving her to it.

MAPOTHER: Oh, vested Caiaphas! Oh, kiss of Judas!

CAREY: In fact, it looks like there'll be a pretty wide boycott.

POER: I was afraid of that. But it's not the universal feeling, apparently?

CAREY: Ah no, sir. There's the illegal organizations and the mountainy men. They only see it as a man getting out of jail, and a slap in the eye for the government. So they're all supporting Mapother's Reception Committee.

MAPOTHER: The heart of the people beats true, my dear sir.

POER: Yes. I think I can hear it beating away. (*Distant shouting*)

ANICE (*entering eagerly*): Is that cheering?

CAREY: Yes, ma'am. I think so.

ANICE: Oh, let me see!

CAREY: It's a great day for all, and I'd like to undo the wrong we did the Doctor. I hope, ma'am, you don't think that I did anything more than my duty?

ANICE: Of course not, Sergeant. There's going to be no hard feelings, and we're all going to forget the past year completely.

CAREY: Oh, I'm glad indeed to hear that, ma'am. It's been on my mind this long while.

ANICE: And you, Mr. Poer? Do you want to see Frank too?

POER: I have a cheque here by way of compensation from the State. I thought I would like to deliver it myself.

MAPOTHER: Oh, a noble gesture.

ANICE: I've no doubt Frank will appreciate your intention, Mr. Poer, whether he accepts your money or not. (*The sound of cheering grows louder*)

CAREY: Here they are now. It's the Doctor himself.

MAPOTHER: Tell me, my good policeman. Can you by any chance discern the sound of a band?

CAREY: No. There's no band.

MAPOTHER: No band! Oh, a mortifying omission! What a reception, and no band!

CHAVASSE (*off*): Thank you, gentlemen. Your welcome touches me more than I can say. It restores all my faith in my fellow men to find that wrong cannot pass unchallenged by people of spirit such as you. (*The cheering swells up and* CHAVASSE *enters, somewhat flushed and excited*)

CHAVASSE: Anice! At last!

ANICE: Frank.

CHAVASSE (*to the others*): What are you all doing here? Please get out.

MAPOTHER: My dear Doctor, as Secretary of the Municipal Welcome Home Committee . . .

CHAVASSE: It's all right, Dominick. I don't mean you. It's these other people.

CAREY: I have some letters and papers to leave in for you, sir.

CHAVASSE: Then leave them. And good afternoon.

CAREY: Yes, sir. (*He pauses in the doorway.*) I am glad to see you back, sir.

CHAVASSE: That will be all, if you please.

CAREY: Yes, sir.

ANICE: Thank you, Sergeant.

CAREY: Thank *you* Miss. (*He goes*)

MAPOTHER: My dear sir, as Secretary and Organizer of the aforementioned Committee it will be my proud privilege to deliver an address of welcome on behalf of the people of this town. But before doing so there is a mortifying gap in the arrangements that must first be obliterated.

CHAVASSE: That's all right, Dominick. I'm very grateful to all my friends.

MAPOTHER: No sir. The proceedings are inadequate without the uplifting strains of appropriate music. I therefore declare them adjourned for a quarter of an hour, when with the indulgence of Providence and the assistance of a battering ram, that want will be supplied. Excuse me, my dear sir. (*He goes out*)

ANICE: Frank, I'm awful. I wanted to have the house in order, but we've only done the hall, and hardly begun on the—

CHAVASSE: And when may we expect Mr. Poer to take a hint?

POER: I realize that you have been through a great deal, Dr. Chavasse. But I am sorry to find that you have taken it badly.

CHAVASSE: Indeed! And how did you expect me to take it?

ANICE: Oh, Frank!

CHAVASSE: The greater part of a year in jail . . . my practice ruined and my health broken down . . . my good name dragged in the mire and a hangman's rope dangled before my face month after month. And at the end, what? A pardon! A pardon, if you please, for a crime I never committed. And now you're sorry to find that I take it badly!

POER: To pardon, after having made a mistake, is a quaint affectation of the law. I realize that. But it's only a formula.

CHAVASSE: A formula to cloak the failure of a lot of malignant spite.

ANICE: Come on, Frank. Let Mr. Poer go. We've so much to talk about ourselves.

POER: Believe me, Doctor, when I say that there was no spite whatever. I have come to tell you that on behalf of myself and also on behalf of Mr. Ua Caoilte, who is no longer in the Government service . . .

CHAVASSE: That's a good beginning, anyhow.

POER: . . . but who has asked me nevertheless to express his best wishes on your release. I hope you understand that whatever mistakes we may have made, we were only trying to carry out our public duties.

CHAVASSE: You mean that you did what you are paid to do—the reckless persecution of innocent men. (ANICE *turns away*)

POER (*stiffening*): Quite so, Doctor. That, of course, is what we are paid to do. And now, before I go, I have to offer you a small sum by way of compensation, which it's usual to give in these circumstances. I thought that it would be a good thing to bring it down personally, but I daresay I was wrong. (*He presents an envelope to* CHAVASSE, *who tears it open and produces a cheque*)

CHAVASSE: A thousand pounds! Well, isn't that nice! A thousand pounds for the ruin of my character and twelve months in jail!

ANICE: Oh Frank! can't you let him go?

CHAVASSE: The law welcomes me home again with a thousand pounds in one hand, and what, I wonder, in the other? (*Opening the letters on the table.*) Tradesmen's bills—four quarters' rent in arrear—law costs—and yes, just as I expected—Income Tax over the past year. I knew I could rely on that! By the way, I hope tax has been deducted from the thousand pounds, or do I include that in my next year's return? (POER *smiles wryly*)

ANICE (*to* POER): Can't you please go away? I can't bear this.

CHAVASSE: Oh, but it's clearly taxable. I've earned it, haven't I? I've provided the fun and now the State is going to pay me for it.

ANICE: He's admitted he was wrong.

POER: It is quite understandable for him to be upset, Miss Hollingshead. It'll be all right later on.

CHAVASSE: Oh no it won't, Poer. You think you can buy me off, but you can't. That's a bigger mistake than the one you made before. I'm taking your cheque, and after I've paid all these things, would you like to know how I intend to spend the balance, if any? In having you charged with malicious prosecution and in seeing that you're properly shown up.

POER: That would be an exceedingly silly waste of money.

CHAVASSE: Oh no, it wouldn't. Mary Quirke is in jail where she ought to be, and Ua Caoilte has been thrown out of his job. That still leaves you, Mr. State Solicitor. And I and my good friends will get you yet.

POER: Don't be a fool, Chavasse. Don't let that gathering of all the cranks and crooks in town persuade you into the belief that you're a public hero.

CHAVASSE: Yes. That is the way you would describe those who hate injustice enough to make a protest about it.

POER: You're in for a big disappointment, Chavasse, if you imagine that those blackguards outside care a rap for justice or injustice. There isn't a mother's son in your whole shock brigade would give a tinker's damn for anything that doesn't concern himself, or can't be turned to political profit. The world is full of injustice . . . worse than you ever suffered, because yours can be repaired. Go and scream about that if you hate injustice. I was sorry for you, Chavasse, but I'm not sorry for you any longer. I've cleaned up my side of this affair, and you can take any steps you like now and go to Hell for all I care.

CHAVASSE: That is all I have to say to you, Poer.

POER: The only person I have any sympathy for now is this lady here, who has been through three times the hell you've ever suffered, and whose only reaction was to downface me in my office and get you out. (CHAVASSE *stalks furiously into the sitting-room*)

ANICE: Oh God, what brought you here again? I knew when I saw you at the door that somehow or other you'd manage to tear all the joy out of everything! Why can't you leave us alone?

POER: I'm sorry, Doctor. But the facts of life are not of my making. And you're surely not one to want to live in a fool's paradise.

ANICE: If you've got to fight with Frank you can at least leave me out of it.

POER: I wish to God you could be left out of it, Miss Hollingshead. It was easy to put Chavasse back where we found him. But there's nothing we can do for you.

ANICE: Thank you, Mr. Poer, but I can face it. You should save your sympathy for those who find it more difficult.

POER: I give my sympathy to those that deserve it.

ANICE: Those that don't deserve it are the only ones who really need it. Can't you see that?

POER: No. I'm afraid I can't.

ANICE: Charity for the rich and sympathy for the strong. That's your creed. But no mercy for the unfortunates who go to bits under suffering—for the weak ones who always get into trouble trying to do strong things. They can hang themselves and welcome. That's justice.

POER: Oh, come. Sometimes I think that justice or injustice doesn't really make much difference in the long run. At least not to people like you and me.

ANICE: That's why you ought to run your racket for the other ones —the ones who are their own worst enemies—the ones that no rules or safeguards can protect.

POER (*after a pause*): I see what you mean.

ANICE: Poor Frank. I'd almost forgotten what he was like until you made him remind me. That was a cruel thing to do. It'll take me a long time to forgive you that.

POER: I'm sorry. But perhaps my coming down here to-day hasn't been so fruitless after all. Do you think that as enemies we might shake hands before I go? (*She gives him her hand silently*) I suppose you'll marry him now. But it's a pity. A great pity. (*She turns away abruptly and* CHAVASSE *enters.* POER *goes. From outside there is a short burst of booing*)

CHAVASSE: Why did you shake hands with him?

ANICE: Somebody had to. After what he did.

CHAVASSE: Do? What did he do?

ANICE: He did what was perhaps the hardest thing of all. In spite of his belief that we were both guilty, he never closed his ears to the other side. He wasn't afraid to prove himself wrong and to make a public admission of his mistake. Was that nothing? And you praise Mapother for your release! Oh, God, it makes me sick to hear you!

CHAVASSE: Anice, why are you talking like that? You haven't taken his side against me?

ANICE: There aren't really any sides. Only different kinds of people.

CHAVASSE: Let all this be. We must get back to security. Security is every thing. We must restore our practice and build up a decent bank balance. We must work together and forget that this hell ever was . . .

ANICE: We shall never forget.

CHAVASSE: Have I not the right to forget? Have I not suffered enough? You, too?

ANICE: Only enough to know how often it happens when nobody listens, nobody hears.

CHAVASSE: Who heard me, will you tell me? (*She turns a little from him. He regards her a little puzzled and moves to her*) But come, let us put it away . . . You go on torturing yourself. You need rest and quiet. (NURSE *enters with* LAURA. *The child is sobbing*)

CHAVASSE: Well, my little Laura, how sweet you look! And dear me, the great big girl you are getting! (*He lifts her up and kisses her.*) What's this? Tears? What is the matter darling?

LAURA: I'm not a thief, daddy. I'm not. I'm not.

CHAVASSE (*setting her down*): Thief? Gracious, what is this? Who said you were a thief?

LAURA (*points to nurse*): She said it. She did, she did.

CHAVASSE: What on earth is all this about, nurse?

NURSE: But this all happened yesterday, doctor, and it was all over, until she suddenly began to cry again a moment ago.

CHAVASSE (*testily*): But what happened? Explain yourself.

NURSE: It was at the children's home where Laura shared a room with another little girl who was given a bar of chocolate for being very good. The chocolate was missing and Laura was blamed.

LAURA (*sobbing*): But I didn't steal it. I didn't. I didn't.

CHAVASSE: You're sure it could only have been Laura?

NURSE: We found her hands all sticky with chocolate, sir.

CHAVASSE (*regarding child severely*): Laura, your father is very disgusted and ashamed of you. He runs home happily to see you and here you are, not only a little thief but a little liar which is worse.

LAURA: But I didn't steal it, daddy, I'm not lying. I'm not. I'm not.

CHAVASSE: You can be stubborn too, I see. I am disgusted with you.

Nurse, she will be sent to bed for this, and she is not to see me again today.

LAURA (*stamping foot and sobbing*): But I'm telling the truth, and you're not fair.

CHAVASSE (*sternly*): Go with the nurse at once.

NURSE: Come, Laura. (LAURA *her lips set evenly, marches off determinedly without looking back to her father.* ANICE *has been standing silently, watching* CHAVASSE *intently. Her face has been masklike, but her eyes amazed and cold*)

CHAVASSE (*turning to her*): You see how the qualities of that—that woman can live on—like a cancer.

ANICE (*coldly*): I didn't think ever that you could have said that.

CHAVASSE: Damnit, Anice, am I a fool? Have I suffered for nothing that I don't know what is plain?

ANICE (*calmly*): Are you sure that the child stole the chocolate?

CHAVASSE: Sure! My God, were you deaf? They found the chocolate stains on her hands!

ANICE: They did. The same forces also found a bottle of poison in your hands. You have not learned much after all, Frank.

CHAVASSE (*looking at her*): You are strange to me, Anice. . . . Perhaps you are right and I was overhasty with the child. I shall see to it. Come, it is a trifle after all.

ANICE: Is it a trifle?

CHAVASSE (*touching her*): Come Anice, these little things will . . . readjust themselves. The flesh creeps over a wound again, and the blood forgets . . . Isn't that it? Darling, it is so long since I've kissed you . . . so long since. . . . (*He places his two hands on her shoulders and draws her to himself.* ANICE *is cold, and her body subtly refuses itself*)

ANICE (*moving away slyly*): Please, Frank—not now. I—I am not sure. . . .

CHAVASSE (*searchingly*): What is it, Anice? You must tell me. You are so cold.

ANICE (*wearily*): I don't know . . . All these months I have dreamed of this moment with longing. You and I free, together, under one roof, and the patients coming and going. . . .

CHAVASSE: But darling, it has come. The door is open and we are going in, with sun streaming after us.

ANICE: But there is something still crashing, breaking into little pieces and floating away . . . I could bear the rest but not it—not it.

CHAVASSE: Echoes—mere echoes.

ANICE: These are not echoes.

CHAVASSE: Anice, you amaze me. What thing is this you say is crashing?

ANICE: I implore you, leave me alone.

CHAVASSE: But I must know. It is my right.

ANICE: It is you! You! Oh, God!

CHAVASSE: Anice! (*He catches her arm*) You must hold on to yourself. I beg of you.

ANICE: Don't touch me or I'll scream! I—I can't bear your touch. (*They break apart*)

CHAVASSE (*slowly*): Then—you don't love me?

ANICE (*slowly*): No . . . and I'll never love you again. . . . Even if I could take those little pieces of you and put them together, I wouldn't want to. . . . Oh, Frank, I must say what I must . . .

CHAVASSE: You are mad, Anice, mad!

ANICE: No . . . I *was* mad. All this time since we've met again, I have been mad—mad in the way that only a woman can be mad. But now I am sane. Now I can add and subtract again. Now I can look out of the window and see what is really there. I have fooled, not you, but myself and I have paid for it.

CHAVASSE: Anice, I will not listen to you now. You are unnerved and overtaxed. We shall discuss all this after you have rested.

ANICE: No. People who discuss things first pull down the blinds of their windows in case they see. I will never pull down the blinds of my windows any more. I see now what I see and God help me. I see you, a free man, gloating over hapless idiots like Mary Quirke and Ua Caoilte, threatening Poer, making cheap bombastic speeches about right and justice and liberty to a petty crowd who know neither right nor justice nor liberty, strutting like a cock in a farmyard and thinking only of your trivial affair. . . . Such is the strange man I see coming to my window and I have no longer love for him, Frank.

CHAVASSE: Surely you know these things you speak of only showed my resentment against injustice. It is human to be resentful.

ANICE: Maybe so. I don't blame you for being yourself. Neither must you blame *me* for being *myself*. I loved you, Frank, when you were being wronged, when you were facing heavy odds. But now that you are free, and now that the battle is over and the blood and sweat have not cleaned you, I love you no longer. You are to me a strange man with whom I will not consort.

CHAVASSE: But you loved me once, Anice. I know you did.

ANICE: I loved you, Frank, back in Innisfree, but perhaps love too can be poisoned out of a black bottle and can die. . . .

CHAVASSE: You are hard on me, Anice. To think for months I dreamed of you and wanted you, with a noose round my neck, and my feet by an open grave and my hands clutching iron bars.

ANICE: I know all that and my heart knows it too. But it makes no difference. I too, was in jail, Frank, and my cell was more horrible than yours. You were alone, wrapped in your agony and protected by it, but my cell was inhabited by ten thousand others with terrible pointing fingers, outcasts like me. And we shared each other. We lent each other our eyes to see with and to cry with. It was then I wakened up out of insanity, and became sane. I could even put my cheek against those iron bars that were more real than yours and smile. One day, Frank, you will borrow the eyes of another, of someone like Mary Quirke or Poer or Ua Caoilte and you'll smile too, but not in the stupid way you smiled today at that cheap mob out there. (*Pause*) Good-bye, Frank. I am going away.

CHAVASSE: You can't go, Anice, and you know you can't. What are you going to do?

ANICE: I don't know. But I know what I *can't* do. Perhaps some day if I am worthy of it, I shall learn what I ought to do. (*She crosses*) Once I loved you, Frank—so much, that at times I really could have killed your wife. . . . Maybe I am guilty after all. . . . I don't know . . . I must work it out . . . (*She goes away. A band is heard approaching in the street. It is a peculiar band, apparently consisting of a piccolo, a bassoon and a big drum. It grows louder and louder as the curtain falls.*)